Keeping the Peace

Keeping the Peace

Practicing Cooperation and Conflict Resolution with Preschoolers

Susanne Wichert

New Society Publishers
Philadelphia, PA and Gabriola Island, BC

Library of Congress Cataloging-in-Publication Data

Wichert, Susanne.
    Keeping the peace : practicing cooperation and conflict resolution with preschoolers /
    Susanne Wichert.
        xi, 98 p. : ill. ; 28 cm.
    Includes bibliographical references (p. 94-97).
    ISBN: 0-86571-158-5 (pbk). ISBN: 0-86571-157-7 (hard).
    1. Education, Preschool--Activity programs. 2. Conflict Management--Study and
    teaching (Preschool). I. Wichert, Susanne. II. Title.
LB1140.35.C74 W53 1989   372.21--dc20   90-110623

Inquiries regarding requests to reprint all or part of *Keeping the Peace* should be addressed to:
    New Society Publishers
    4527 Springfield Avenue
    Philadelphia, PA 19143

ISBN USA 0-86571-157-7 Hardcover
ISBN USA 0-86571-158-5 Paperback
ISBN CAN 1-55092-030-8 Hardcover
ISBN CAN 1-55092-031-6 Paperback

Cover and book design by Tina Birky.

front cover   Photographed by Susanne Wichert at The Willows. Children pictured are Patrick
                Kumai-Scott and Jack Shapiro.
page 7   Photographed by Marta Reinhart at Germantown Friends School Nursery Program.
page 33   Photographed by Esther Cristol at Germantown Friends School Nursery Program.
page 59   Photographed by Joan Bobrow at Germantown Friends School Nursery Program.
page 93   Photographed by Marta Reinhart at Germantown Friends School Nursery Program.
back cover   Photographed by Beth Durant at Germantown Friends School Nursery Program.

To order directly from the publisher, add $2.50 to the price for the first copy, 75¢ each additional. Send check
or money order to:
    New Society Publishers
    4527 Springfield Avenue
    Philadelphia, PA 19143
In Canada, contact:
    New Society Publishers/New Catalyst
    PO Box 189
    Gabriola Island, BC VOR 1XO

New Society Publishers is a project of the New Society Educational Foundation, a nonprofit, tax-exempt,
public foundation in the United States, and of the Catalyst Education Society, a non-profit society in Canada.
Opinions expressed in this book do not necessarily represent positions of the New Society Educational
Foundation, nor the Catalyst Education Society.

Table of Contents

Acknowledgments

Remember the famous scene from some old movie where Mickey Rooney says, "Hey gang . . . let's put on a show!"? Well, in my case there were those who said (with enthusiasm, mind you), "Hey . . . let's make a preschool/daycare where we teach children conflict resolution and all that other good stuff!" I want to thank them all, and especially Amy Hagopian, for that early inspiration.

The Willows, the place where all these ideas came to life, was a place I shared for five years with the best friend and business partner of all time, Randi Solinsky. We shared that first moment when we stood in a classroom and were not needed because the children were managing their problems themselves and having fun doing it. I remember we looked at each other and said, "Gee, this stuff really works!"

We also shared the hard times when both toilets backed up and up and up and flooded the whole classroom. Because Randi was there, I survived—and did it laughing.

Of the ideas in this book that are original, not one of them would be here if it weren't for Randi. Even though she may have been generous enough to allow me to write them down, which allows me to call this "my" book—it isn't. There are whole hunks of R. S. in here. I'll bet she's been wondering where she left them!

Many thanks also to Margie Carter who has been an inspiration and support through the last five years and who is singly responsible for this manuscript ever seeing the inside of a publishing office.

Thanks also to Renée Motley, the first Willows staff member (besides us), who willingly tried out activities that we made up. The ones included in this book all worked, but Renée also had to try a bunch of the ones that didn't. I learned a lot from Renée.

I also wish to express my gratitude to the Pacific Peace Fund, whose original grant allowed me to buy some of the time to write this, and to all the parents who supported us through the years, especially Valerie Trueblood and Rick Rapport.

Then there's my husband, James Kairoff, who typed for me when my back hurt, patiently explained to me the basics of how to use this stupid word processor and continues to tell me how clever I am. Thanks also to my stepson Joshua Kairoff for giving me the computer in the first place.

Special thanks must go to the people who have staffed The Willows through the years, who not only shared the vision, but brought it to life. Last but not least, what would it be without the children?

I wish to dedicate this work to the memory of my mother, Elfriede H. Wichert whose suffering during World War II has made me strive to work for a world in which nobody has to fear violence. I'm pleased to be finishing this on what would have been her seventy-sixth birthday.

29 December, 1988

Preface

The material in this book comes from a variety of sources including that vast storehouse of teachers' and caregivers' tricks and ideas that exists wherever people care for and about young children. My attempt to organize the old ideas and develop new ideas was made possible in a wonderful laboratory called "The Willows."

The Willows was a preschool/daycare program created and operated by Randi Solinsky and myself. We ran it for five years from the fall of 1983 to the fall of 1988 in Seattle, Washington. Much of the credit for our five successful years must go to the dedication of our staff and the support of the parents whose children were enrolled. All the ideas in this book were tested out in a real daycare setting (where you have to continue to operate even though half the staff is out sick and the toilets just backed up to flood the whole classroom). They work.

When Randi and I started The Willows, our primary objectives were:

—to develop a quality preschool daycare program committed to an active interpretation of humanistic values;

—to have a strong, *age appropriate* conflict resolution component as part of the program;

—to involve parents in a number of ways, with a special emphasis on giving parents the opportunity to subject their own ideas about violence and war to scrutiny, particularly regarding parenting.

In trying to tailor a daycare program to meet these objectives (with affordability an ever-present concern), we were compelled to look at many areas, including our daily interaction with children and each other, as well as to the development of specific activities designed to teach the components of cooperative behavior.

Evaluating our success in an objective and quantifiable way has been difficult due to the abstract definitions of behavior with which we are dealing. It is our subjective opinion that we have had an impressive measure of success. We noticed an increase in altruistic behavior and an observable decrease in aggressive behavior. We were able to integrate some children who had specific problems with aggression into our classrooms and have seen the incidence of their aggressive behavior diminish. In addition, we noticed a seemingly greater tolerance among children for the differences in others. It would also seem that children carried these skills with them when they left us for other settings. We have heard from parents that their children's new teachers have commented on the "diplomatic" role these children assumed in resolving conflicts both with and among other children.

Last, but certainly not least, we all enjoyed working in the classroom more than ever before.

It is my hope that this information is useful not just to teachers and caregivers, but also to parents. I think the ideas presented work just as well in a family or play-group setting as in a classroom. Or if your child is in daycare, encourage your caregiver to try out some of these ideas and support them in their attempts.

There is so much more that could have gone into this book, but some of that has already been written, and I encourage you to read those books as well. I wish you peace and love and success.

"Peace is not the absence of conflict. Conflict is an inevitable fact of daily life—internal, interpersonal, intergroup and international conflict. Peace consists in creatively dealing with conflict. Peace is the process of working to resolve conflicts in such a way that both sides win, with increased harmony as the outcome of the conflict and its resolution. The resolution is peaceful if the participants come to want to cooperate more fully and find themselves enabled to do so."

—Jim and Kathy McGinnis, *Parenting for Peace and Justice*

Introduction

Our society has changed a lot in the last century and seems destined to continue to do so at an alarming rate. Yet in all this change, some things remain the same. We all want our children to grow up into happiness and peace, with a strong sense of values and the courage to make moral choices. While we may differ on the finer points, we can probably all agree that we hope for children who grow up to be kind and fair.

Many of the values that people carry through their lives have their beginnings early in life. Sadly, in an increasingly violent world, parents and teachers of young children often fail to address the issues of conflict and violence. Just as violence has become a seemingly acceptable part of children's culture in this society, so we must confront those ideas, call them what they are, and help our children learn an alternative view of the world and the skills to make that alternative a part of their lives.

We must empower them to make choices about right and wrong and to have the courage to stand up for their convictions. By failing to address the issues of violence, ethnocentric distortions, mutual distrust, and mutual isolation, we fail to teach children the very things they will need to take charge and shape their lives and the world.

Taking Charge

Jesse started second grade in a new school, and children were still settling into social groupings. He had been at The Willows for two of his preschool years and, even though he loved to goad his mother by asking for guns in front of guests, had strong feelings about the use of violence. It was therefore a big problem for him when a fourth grade boy began to wait for him in the hall and pick on him, threatening him and pushing him around. He attempted to respond in a number of ways for the following two weeks. He tried talking to the boy, asking him why he was doing this, and offering to do favors for him. Jesse was very sympathetic to the boy, assuming that things must be pretty bad for him, and that maybe if he tried being his friend it would help matters. The boy spurned his offers and increased his bullying. We talked about his going to some of the teachers, but there were several reasons why this was not a solution to the problem. First of all, the teachers believed that children needed to work these things out among themselves; and second, it was an

1

alternative school where children had a great deal of freedom of movement, and it was virtually impossible to monitor closely.

Jesse and I had a number of conversations about this problem. Throughout, I was struck by his continuing desire to understand the other boy's perspective, and by his continuing attempts at nonviolent solutions. When he had been in my classroom, I could control the environment so nonviolent solutions worked. But there he was, out in the real world where things aren't quite so simple. I could only be there to support whatever decision he made.

After attempting everything he could think of, including trying to avoid the boy, Jesse made the decision to confront him. He made one last attempt to reason with him and them told him in no uncertain terms that if he (the older boy) continued to bully him, he would hurt him back. Sadly, the older boy's response was to laugh and push him on the stairs, so Jesse followed through on his threat and kicked him in the shin. This resolved the problem and the older boy left Jesse alone from then on.

Even though the ultimate solution involved violence, I felt very proud of the way Jesse had handled himself. He never felt good about hurting the other boy, although he was relieved when the abuse stopped. We cannot always keep our children out of situations like this one, but we can help them face such problems with compassion and a bag of tricks greater than just hitting back. He has taken charge in his world.

One frequent activity in my classroom was altering freely stories we read to children. Hence, we often changed the gender of a character to even things out, rather than avoid a book that might otherwise be good. We were very open with children about this process, sometimes giving them choices.

Phoebe was five years old and had been at The Willows for two years. In addition, her mother had a strong commitment to nonviolence and the elimination of gender bias. One night Phoebe was staying the night at my house and had brought along *Winnie the Pooh*, which her mother was reading to her at bedtime, one chapter a night. When it was time to read the chapter for the night, Phoebe told me which chapter I should read and explained to me that I had to change all the characters to girls, except for Christopher Robin, who could remain a boy. She has taken charge in her world.

David and Jason were both at a table playing side by side with Legos. Both were quietly building until David made a gun out of the Legos, pointed it at Jason, and made shooting noises. Jason looked up from what he was building and said, "I don't like it when you shoot me. Please stop." He has taken charge in his world.

Natasha was in tenth grade when she decided to take an electronics class. Most of the other students in this class were boys and the teacher was male. The main items of decor in the classroom were posters from various electronics suppliers, one of them depicting a young woman in a skimpy outfit. She didn't need to talk it over with anyone. It was very clear to her what she needed to do, so she went to the instructor and, without being confrontational, explained that the poster was demeaning to women and made her uncomfortable and asked him to remove it. He did. She has taken charge in her world.

Starting Early

These stories are examples of children of varying ages who have gained the ability to make value judgments about fairly common events in their lives and the confidence to act on them. How did they get there and what can you as a parent or caregiver do to help children on a day-to-day basis?

There are currently "values education" programs available for use with children in elementary and secondary school. The amount they are used varies from school to school and teacher to teacher. These programs are very useful and I commend teachers and parents for using them. Unfortunately, however, not only do we need to develop approaches for use with much younger children, but we need to take a look at what we do and say *every day* that influences children. The material in this book is designed for use with preschool-aged children. While it has been specifically tested out in a classroom setting, it can also be used in play-group and family situations.

Goals and scope of this book

In order for children to engage repeatedly in constructive conflict resolution, the following needs to happen:

>—the amount of conflict in the environment must be fairly low, so that . . .
>—the adult can guide the resolution process where necessary, so that . . .
>—the resolution process works for, and not against the child, thereby encouraging the child to use it again.

I start out, in "The Setting," considering the environment. In the largest sense, this means considering the goals and values that we bring to the endeavor. More specifically, there are ways we can arrange the physical environment, in terms of space and equipment, that enhance the qualities required for successful conflict resolution and minimize unnecessary conflict. Finally, I consider the limits we want to set, the objects and behaviors we want to screen out of the environment.

Even more important than the setting is the quality of adult attention and interaction with children. In the second section, "Interacting with Children," I discuss the daily role adults can play in helping children develop the wide array of attitudes and skills necessary for conflict resolution. The final section, "Activities," consists of a series of formal group activities with the same goal.

Through this book, you should be better able to help the children in your life learn to manage many of the conflicts they face in their lives. The ability to do that successfully will reinforce their self-confidence and enable them to take on even more difficult situations.

There is violence and conflict in our children's experience, however, that this appoach cannot fully address. While a child who has been badly abused will certainly be helped by a context that nurtures self-esteem and respect, the internal conflict and pain that child faces will not be addressed by better communication or negotiating skills. A child who is deeply and chronically angry at his or her lack of power in the face of an adult-controlled environment may not be appeased by small tokens of power within that context.

We must not pretend we are solving all of a child's problems-this can be very confusing for children. But we can help. The amount of unresolved conflict in any setting can be reduced by creating an environment where people feel more comfortable, valued as individuals, respected; where they can be free to express their feelings, and are more assured of getting what they need. Even though you may work with children in a setting where conflict is high, and where you don't have much support or control over the environment, you *can* create positive change. It may take time, but *there will be change*.

The Larger View

It is my goal in writing this book to provide detailed and useful information about how children can be helped to develop skills that allow them to practice conflict resolution.

All these tools are useless, however, unless they are practiced with a larger view in mind. It is essential that children be in a milieu that reflects greater peace and justice issues in every way possible.

Children need to be treated with respect and be accepted for who they are even if this sometimes doesn't mesh with what we would like to see them be. They need to be validated and affirmed, and to see us validate and affirm each other. Our discipline for them should be nonpunitive and nonhumiliating, and come from the place in our hearts where we treasure them.

Children need to learn about and see us practice respect for people who are different and people who stand for social justice and peace.

Children should be allowed to grow up into their full potential and not be restricted to the notion of what we think they should be.

Children should experience love and not see us be embarrassed by it.

Children need to see us value our ideas and actions that make up our striving for peace and justice and be encouraged to participate. As we stretch to offer all of this to children, our lives—as well as theirs—will become richer, and the world will be that much safer for all of us.

The Setting

I

The setting for the children we raise, care for, or teach is influenced in the larger sense by the objectives and values we bring to that time together, as well as by the environment we create around us. For many of us, especially parents, these issues stay on an intuitive or subconscious level most of the time. But bringing them out in the open and examining them helps us to be clearer and more powerful in the choices we make.

1
Establishing Objectives

Establishing our objectives is important, because they define the communal effort and help us to set priorities. It is very easy to fall in the trap of defining a program by what it does *not* do rather than by what it does. How many programs would state as their objectives that they teach racism, sexism, and violence? I believe that in order to teach humanistic values to chidren, it is essential to become active about the interpretation of ideas, rather than just reactive when we see something offensive or troubling.

The following list of objectives reflects the intertwined relationship between self-esteem, tolerance of difference, creative problem-solving, altruism, and the ability to deal nonaggressively with problems. These objectives are meant to serve as guidelines for setting your own program goals.

1.1 Sample program objectives

1. Give children opportunities to develop positive self-esteem, including opportunities for increasing competence.
2. Foster and encourage the development of altruistic, caring behavior.
3. Foster understanding and tolerance for differences, including the development of a global view of the world, with respect for other cultures and traditions.
4. Teach children to value all life and abhor the purposeful taking of it.
5. Teach children to express and value their own feelings and the feelings of others.
6. Teach children how to resolve conflicts in a nonviolent way.
7. Provide children with experiences that demonstrate the multiplicity of solutions to a problem.
8. Have fun and laugh a lot.

If you run a program, it is important to develop objectives and review them periodically with all staff, and parents if appropriate, in order to achieve a unity of vision, organization, and purpose. We have found it works best to run our classrooms cooperatively, with all staff involved in setting objectives and priorities (while picking joyful tangents along the way), and developing ideas to help us meet them.

If you are a head teacher in a classroom, it is important to have your objectives clearly in mind and periodically measure the activities in your classroom against them. Your clarity will allow other adults in the classroom to better mesh with you and enhance your efforts.

If your child is in a daycare center, preschool, or play-group, you should understand the program objectives of that group in order to be supportive and accountable. There are often many ways parents can enhance the values and ideas children are learning in the classroom. If you don't know how, ask!

If you are a parent shopping for a care situation, be prepared to interview the staff about all manner of issues. Just as you would ask about what kind of snacks are served, you should feel free to ask about the kinds of values that are acted out. It might be helpful to answer a few of the questions about "What do you think?" and "What do you do when?" from the following chapter, "Personal Values Clarification." In addition, take time to observe the classroom setting long enough to see the staff handle the more difficult parts of the day. Do not assume that because people mean well they are able to act in ways that match your values. (Please, however, be merciful and nondisruptive—and if you like what you see, tell them!)

1.2 When objectives are in conflict

While it can be a fairly straightforward process to develop these objectives, any group of people can run into problems when we begin to talk about how we will work ideas into practice. It is important to take that next step, because it will help you clarify what, in fact, you want to have happen.

On occasion, some of these ideas will seem to be in conflict and it may take a great deal of thought and patience to resolve the situation without compromising any principles. Let me give you an example:

I decided in one of my classrooms that the children had very limited experience with older people, and that this limited exposure was affecting the children's attitudes about age. I already had classroom materials that included positive images of the elderly, so I devoted my energy to including older people in the classroom. Attempts to bring in grandparents, directly and indirectly, helped somewhat, but again, I found the results limited.

I decided to enlist some elderly volunteers. Perhaps I was just unlucky, but I found that the three volunteers who came my way all brought prejudices that ended up causing problems, especially around sexism. Though they meant well, the issue seemed to manifest itself in a hundred different small ways. I was uncomfortable, feeling I had no right to demand that these volunteers change the beliefs and habits of a lifetime, but not wanting those prejudices played out in my classroom. Ultimately, I managed to work this out by attempting to deal honestly and with respect with each individual. In some instances I was understood; in some instances, I was not.

Another similar example again pitted sexism against cultural difference. We often ran into the situation where, in an attempt to talk about a different culture, the materials available depicted rigid sex stereotyping. We didn't want to "censor" a culture, yet were very uncomfortable with the inherent sexism. As you can imagine, long and sometimes heated debates arose from this issue.

So as you can see, continuing discussion seems to be required. It has been my experience that if you hold on to your objectives and deal honestly and cooperatively, a reasonable solution can be found.

2
Personal Values Clarification

Children come into the world with a strong capacity for altruism and empathy, and are strongly affected by their very early experiences. They are exposed to much in the way of values education and training during preschool years. Sadly, much of this is by way of default, when we don't consciously examine the things we do and say.

As a result, our children get many confusing and mixed values messages: when we encourage them not to throw away food, since it is of great value—particularly to those who don't have enough—yet we use cornmeal or beans for play; when we admire girls for how nice they look and say nothing to boys; when we reinforce consumerism by carrying on about somebody's new sneakers; when the only pictures of Africa we show to children are all tribal pictures; when we are intolerant of a child who is different or messy; when we allow children to see us use another person as something to be manipulated to get what we want.

In order for you as a teacher or parent to consciously influence the values of young children, you must first be very clear about your own, as well as the strenth and form of your commitment. You must also understand how values are passed on, both directly and indirectly, and learn to communicate well about these issues. It won't be enough to say "X is bad"—children need to understand your reasons to make sense of your values. This examination of our values in action can be difficult and even tiresome, but we owe the children in our care this kind of consciousness. Your own conviction is the most effective tool you have, and without it, you will accomplish little.

Being with children can often place adults in a situation where one principle is pitted against another and we are forced to choose. It is important to make these choices consciously. It may also be helpful to share your thinking process with the child.

Jan had three children and had always tried to give her children everything they needed, but not everything they wanted. She felt very strongly that even though they led a middle-class lifestyle, her children should understand

11

that they could be happy without having all the material possessions they might ask for. She had successfully gotten through any number of current crazes in kiddie consumerism and felt comfortable with how she had done it. Now, however, she was not sure what to do. Her daughter Sally, who was in second grade this year, had a difficult time the year before, not making friends easily and often excluded at school. This year Sally had made friends with two other girls and was feeling considerably better.

One day Sally asked to have a certain kind of pencil box. When Jan pointed out that she had a pencil box already, Sally explained that the other two girls had a special kind of pencil box and they wanted to make a club which hinged on this item. Jan wasn't sure what to do. On one hand, Sally already had a perfectly good pencil box and it seemed excessive to get another. Besides, she didn't feel very good about the idea of friendship based on the possession of an item. There was also the issue of exclusion to think about. Would they exclude any other children who didn't have one of the pencil boxes?

On the other hand, Sally had felt so badly last year. Was it right to sacrifice her daughter's self-esteem for a principle? The other thing to consider was that Sally had been honest about why she wanted it and had not pretended to have lost it like she might have done.

Jan decided to talk with her daughter about those issues. She shared her concerns and then asked Sally to think about it herself for a day. Jan told Sally that she would let her decide and would respect her decision.

Although there could have been many possible solutions, Sally chose to talk to her friends the next day about exclusion, friendship and money, as she had with her mother. The three of them decided the pencil box rule was not good, and dropped it. Then they asked a fourth girl to join their club.

You may or may not agree with what Jan decided to do. Let's complicate the matter further by changing the problem. What if the item Sally wanted was a toy gun? Would that change your view of the problem? Why?

The process of clarifying your feelings about issues is of necessity an ongoing one. People's feelings about things change through their lives and what they choose to do about them also varies. While just thinking things through is helpful, I have found it much more productive to have other people involved in the process. If you are a teacher, try to get together with other teachers and talk. As a parent, you can use informal or formal times together to talk about values.

The following set of questions, while narrow in focus, can be used as a starting point for discussion and an examination of your parenting or classroom habits. It can be hard, time-consuming work to think about these and similar questions, and you may be tempted to skim this list and continue on. I would encourage you to set some time aside by yourself or with a coworker to clarify your own thinking on these issues. Try to think about these and other questions not only from your perspective, but also from a child's point of view. Also, note any discrepancies between your very best thinking on an issue and your gut feeling. If they are different, children will inevitably pick up both messages, and, unless you've done a good job of explaining, will find it very confusing. Most of all, remember that there are no right or wrong answers; there are only *your* answers.

What do you think?

—Are wars good or bad?
—All, or just some?
—Are there situations which justify war?
—Is war of some kind or another inevitable?
—Are soldiers good or bad?
—What about soldiers in children's stories? What do they do?
—Do kings, queens, and countries always have soldiers? Why?

What do you do when?

—A child is very excited about a new present they've gotten from a relative, and it's a GI Joe lunchbox?
—Several other children cluster around excitedly and examine it?
—Your children and their friends are playing a game that involves shooting and fighting. When confronted, they say, " . . . but we're not really killing. We're just playing."

What do you think?

—Is killing good or bad?
—Are there circumstances in which killing can be justified? If so, what circumstances?
—What does killing actually do to a person?
—What does it do to the person doing the killing?
—What about nonhuman lives?

What do you do when?

—Children are playing some kind of shooting game, and when you intervene, they tell you they are shooting "freezing rays" or "rays that turn the bad guys into good guys"?
—A child tells you about some people who died in a flood, but "they'll be okay, 'cause it was just on TV"?
—The ugliest, hairiest, world's most creepy spider is in your room?

What do you think?

—Do you think aggression is a natural part of the make-up of human beings?
— . . . of *male* human beings?
—Do people have a need to act out aggression?
—Does acting out aggression diminish or enhance the likelihood of further violent behavior on the part of the individual?
—Are there circumstances that make aggression justifiable?

What do you do when?

—You see a quiet, shy child who has been tormented by a bully, finally hit the other child, and both children know that you have seen them?
—A child tells you, " . . . but my daddy says I'm a big boy now and I should know how to fight"?
—A child in dress-up is hitting a doll?

What do you think?

—Is sharing and taking equal-length turns always fair?
—Because somebody owns something, does that give them special rights to it?
—Do people have a right to exclude others from their activities, to choose their associates?
—Is making a child do something they say they don't want to do bad?

What do you do when?

—A lonely child refuses another child's offer to join in a game you know she really likes?
—Two children have made up a special game for themselves and don't want to include a third, who *really* wants to join?
—A child brings in a very attractive (and unbreakable) thing from home for show-and-tell and doesn't want to let anybody else touch it?

You may also find yourself making up more specific hypothetical situations to explain different responses. I think this tends to be a very valuable process, as ultimately every situation you encounter will have its own unique circumstances. Your ability to talk about your feelings and choices to another adult in a discussion situation will help you when the time comes to honestly explain your feelings to a child.

3
Setting Up the Physical Environment

The physical space at your disposal and your use of it is an important factor in the amount of conflict generated. An analysis of it should be one of the first steps you take.

Sadly, we cannot always have the kind of space and equipment we would like. Often, daycare and preschool programs must accept far from adequate housing. It is then left up to staff to compensate for the shortcomings of the facility. Play space at home is often even more limited, calling for greater ingenuity on the part of the parent.

This section is to help you evaluate your facility with a specific focus on the reduction of *nonconstructive* conflict.

3.1 Goals for the environment

Let us start by defining some objectives for the ideal facility. The ideal facility would:

—Allow children to function with the maximum degree of independence. When children are able to do many things for themselves or with the help of another child, not only is there an enhancement of self-esteem and increased opportunity for altruistic behavior, but staff can spend less time on purely custodial tasks. Obviously, the teacher who is freed from these custodial tasks is better able to monitor for conflict and guide it to its resolution.

—Allow all persons in it to function at a low-stress level. A number of physical factors can influence stress level, among them noise level, visual clutter, use of color, and space/child ratio.

—Be as comfortable as possible for a variety of uses. Space in a preschool classroom should aid in establishing a strong link between the parent and the center. With that aim in mind, there should be a number of places where a parent and child can be together comfortably for a while. The parent's comfort and sense of trust is passed on to the child and has a direct influence on the child's ability to feel secure and to view the values expressed at the center as consistent with the values in the child's family. The space should also have a number of "retreats" for children or adults who need some time alone during the day.

15

The choice of equipment is also vitally important. Again, the reality is that few staff working in daycare and preschool settings—and fewer parents— have the opportunity to acquire the kind of equipment they would like to have. It is not always possible for teachers to be involved in setting up budgets and making purchasing decisions. It is worthwhile to make the attempt, however, because a wise choice of equipment that takes a long range view can have a tremendous impact on what happens for children.

Traditionally, the preschool teacher—and, again, the active parent— spends a lot of time scrounging material and developing elaborate schedules designed to keep children from conflicting in an economy of scarcity. Basically, the idea is to change to an economy of surplus without spending a lot of money.

3.2 Thinking about play areas

What follows are some examples of classroom and area analysis. I don't claim that any of these ideas are new or original. What I have tried to do is to look at things with the specific objectives of reducing nonconstructive conflict and increasing situations allowing for guided or constructive conflict resolution. It is also important to evaluate play areas in terms of how well they promote altruistic and inclusive behavior, as well as meet the individual developmental needs of the children who will be using them.

The classroom areas with which I will be dealing are fairly standard for a developmental/interactive classroom model. In the case of a more specialized classroom setting, such as a Waldorf or Montessori classroom, this analysis may not apply as easily.

3.3 A note for parents

While the following discussion is framed in terms of a classroom setting, there are many ideas here that are applicable for home use. As you read, think about the *space* in your house with your children's needs in mind. There are lots of possibilities, many of which we have probably never even considered. Ask yourself about ideas like the following: putting an easy chair in the kitchen; making your living room small and your play space big; all sleeping in one room to free another for activity areas; a loft for private or quiet activity; a special attic hideout?

Think about the *equipment* you want available. Again, as you read on, you will see that there are more workable possibilities than most of us imagine. How about investing in or scrounging for blocks, dress-ups, and craft materials, rather than just toys and books? How about a special table where you control the materials that get put out?

Ask yourself questions about your children, yourself, your objectives: What kind of play do you want to encourage—and what space and equipment will help? Where can you tolerate the most mess, and what implications does that have for hard play or arts and crafts? What organization will give your children maximum independence and accessibility while allowing you the control you need? If the children use particular limited resources hard, how can you expand them?

There are rich possibilities for making the physical environment in our homes even more nourishing of capable, independent, and thoughtful children.

3.4 Dramatic play area

This is the area that is traditionally called "housekeeping" or "the doll corner," and is considered very important for the emotional development of children because it is where they perform family play. It usually consists of a small stove, sink, table, chairs, and dolls as well as miscellaneous props and clothes.

But I have consistently had a number of problems with this set-up, among them a definite rigidity in the kinds of sex roles children were playing out— "You're the girl, so you have to clean the kitchen"—and some difficulty in kindling new interest in the area after the initial burst of play at the start of the year.

In thinking through this, it became apparent that there was no reason to confine objectives to one play area, rather that they could be shuffled together from areas all over the classroom and redealt. It seemed like the kinds of things we wanted to see happen in the building block area, which was an area that attracted boys, and the things we wanted to see happen in housekeeping were very similar, if not the same. It seemed we might have a lot to gain by looking at the secondary equipment in those areas and seeing how it affected the structure of the play.

The opportunities for play in those areas were as follows:

1. Dramatic play of all kinds, fantasy- as well as reality-based;
2. Domestic play, in which children tried out familial roles of various kinds;
3. Cooperative play, and, because of the very interactive nature of this kind of play, many opportunities for resolving conflict creatively;
4. Play in which children could enjoy ornamenting themselves in the most flexible way possible;
5. Play in which children could experience concretely the multicultural aspects of our world.

The first and easiest decision was not to buy a child-sized stove and sink. These items tend to be quite expensive and there were lots of other ways to spend money. However, even if we had been given them, we would not have used them. It was time to go beyond housekeeping . . .   The area was the dress-up area, and it changed character every few months, depending on the children's interest and teachers' energy. This idea was extremely liberating and opened up all kinds of new ways for us to help children find out about the world. It is my belief that domestic play will occur with or without a housekeeping area, and after watching a child sweetly bedding down a doll with a brick for a pillow, I stopped worrying about it all that much. (Please see the "Blocks area" section for a discussion of how we facilitated doll play in that area.)

In going beyond housekeeping, we found ourselves going far out into the world on occasion. Some of the things our dress-up area became were a community clinic, a grocery store, a nonwestern shelter, a rainforest, a stage, and a wildlife preserve. Because the area changed when the children's interest began to flag, they were always pretty anxious to have opportunities to play in the area. Children were involved in working out a way they would all have fair access. In addition, the desirability of the area allowed a certain amount of manipulation on our part.

It is the nature of dramatic play that there is a high level of communication among children as they work out the plots of their game and the drama unfolds, and we as teachers took full advantage. If two children in the classroom were having difficulty getting along, or were simply children who had little to do with each other, we could get them involved with one another by making sure that they were both playing in the area at the same time. Staff remained attentive and helped guide in any conflict that wasn't being handled well by children. This was also a good area for working out issues of exclusion among children. Threesomes often developed in the classroom, in which one of the three children sometimes got pushed out of play. By remaining alert to the opportunity, teachers had lots of chances to help children work through what it feels like to be excluded by each other and to work out alternative ways of playing.

Another advantage of this changeable dress-up area was its tendency to involve parents in the classroom just a little more. Because we didn't want to spend money on this set-up, we needed imagination and help from the parents. This usually took the form of their lending or giving us items, and we always requested that they and the child put the item in the area together. Invariably, they ended up hanging out and having their child show them everything.

Transforming part of your classroom this way can require a certain amount of courage the first time, but I think after you do it once, you'll find it's so much fun—you'll never go back to the old way!

Here's one of our admittedly more unusual ideas: It was a time of year when it rains a lot here in Seattle, and we were spending lots of time inside. I was watching children play and thinking about how my brother and I built houses out of all the blankets and sheets in the house when we were children. Our mother let us keep them up for weeks while we expanded our design. I wanted the children in my class to have that kind of experience. I had attempted putting out blankets and sheets in blocks, but because we used the area during transitions, we never left anything up. I started thinking about using the dress-up area in some way . . .

In the meantime, my two colleagues in the classroom had been thinking about some ways of giving the children more concrete experiences with multicultural ideas. They had overheard some children talking about how people live, and with the absolute certainty only a four-year-old can muster, heard that all people live in houses like theirs.

When we came together for our staff meeting we began to toss ideas around. Ultimately we decided to change the dress-up area into a house, but that it would be a very special place. Our goal was to give the children all the things they would need to construct a shelter they could change around, but the materials would all be materials that people in other parts of the world used for shelter construction. They would also have props to use in this house, but again, all the props would have to be of nonsuburban origin.

We thought for a while about mixing items from different cultures and whether or not that would be confusing. But we decided that if we took the time to tell children about items, it would be alright. Since we wanted to increase the children's understanding about different ways of life, we also decided to do some work in small groups on the topic of *shelter*.

The first thing we did was to spend some short times with the whole group looking at pictures and reading books in which there were different kinds of shelter. We also had a table in the room on which we generally had books for adults with good pictures about some topic which we encouraged children, parents, and teachers to peruse in odd moments. We found, in our local library, lots of wonderful books with marvelous pictures of shelters that people build. Most of us were stunned by the beautiful variety of shelters people build. We found ourselves needing to take great care not to misrepresent a culture. For example, we didn't want children to think that all houses in all of Africa looked like the homes of the Masai. We took care to show pictures of cities as well as more rural areas, as well as some of the great differences from one region to another. This was not difficult, as there really is a lot of pictorial information available. Additionally, we attempted to give children an understanding of the reasons for the differences in how people live. For example, we explained that the Inuit igloo is built from ice rather than thatch because that is the material available. Admittedly, we often found ourselves without a proper answer for a child's question, and had to search for it.

Our next step was to build a lean-to out of sticks on the playground. They were tied together with raffia I'd found at a basketmaking supply store. This took several days and the children were very involved in it.

Next came building a house inside the classroom. We had to abandon my idea of giving the children supplies with which they could build from scratch. I didn't mind. One child had wanted to bring in several square yards of dirt to put on the floor, and she couldn't have her way either. It took us a few tries to figure out exactly how to do it, and it wasn't really pretty when we were done, but we ended up with a frame made out of big sticks on which children could hang various straw mats, a thatch raincape five-feet long, large pieces of felt made earlier in the year, and some lengths of fabric. They had a big wooden bowl full of clothespins (a concession!) which they could use to clip things together.

In the meantime we had sent a note home to parents explaining what we were doing and asking them to send whatever they had. We made it clear that children would be playing vigorously with these items, so it shouldn't be anything precious to them. Fragile items were OK to send for us to look at. The result was wonderful. Parents were telling us that children began to notice things in their own homes and that they were hearing comments like: "That's made out of clay." We certainly had more than we needed. There were batik pillows from Indonesia and some with mirrors embroidered in from India; there were bowls of clay and wood and gourds; there were baskets of all kinds. Most exciting was the selection of clothing. It came from all over, was beautiful, and the children loved it. My favorite day was when some children and a wonderful, patient teacher, Patricia, got interested in how people carry babies around. Patricia knew how to tie a shawl to carry a baby, so there were six children—most of them boys—walking around all day with assorted dolls and animals tied to them. They played with their babies on their backs; they ate lunch with their babies on their backs; they even tried to take naps with their babies on their backs!

That portion of the dress-up area not occupied by the actual shelter or storage became the outside of the house and children had props available to represent activities that might take place outside of someone's house, like gardening. They also had space to build a "fire" if they chose.

Prior to introducing any item to the area, we showed it to the children at group time, explaining its origin and use. We also discussed how it should be handled. Children showed a great deal of respect in handling these things and items were rarely damaged.

This area was set up in our classroom for about ten weeks and we all felt that it had been pretty successful. Prior to this set up, showing a picture of a mud-construction house would have likely elicited the comment, "yucky," but would now bring forth a comment of interest or curiosity instead.

Another important aspect of setting this area up in this way is the possibility for children to participate actively in its creation. No matter what it is we end up creating, it seems that there are always lots of ways for children to participate in making decisions about what to put in, where to put it, and how to make things. When we had a wildlife preserve, the idea had come from the children. They ended up making lots of the vegetation and rocks. When we had a restaurant, children decided on the kind of food they wanted served and then we figured out ways they could make it. When children made things, we were nonjudgmental about it and encouraged children to be accepting of each others' work. In other words, if Patrick said that a bunch of little scraps of paper were fish for the lake—they were. Over time this acceptance of another person's choices and abilities generalized to the rest of the classroom and we heard "that's not the right way" with considerably less frequency. Children also became more likely to make stuff on their own. If they needed a little person for some game and there wasn't one around, they would go to the drawing area and construct something out of paper and tape.

The possibilities are endless. We held a workshop called "Beyond Housekeeping." At the end of two hours, fifteen participants had generated a list of over twenty ideas and had worked out the details for five of them. Think of this as your opportunity to unleash your creative potential.

3.5 Blocks area

Blocks is another high communication area and so can be very fertile ground for fine-tuning communication and negotiation skills. But this area can also be another "gender trap" if you don't keep an eye on it. Having it close to the dress-up area and allowing the movement of props back and forth can help to eliminate some of the gender segregation as well as increase opportunities for cooperative play.

It is the nature of block play to require a fairly large amount of space. Through the years I have often had the blocks area do double duty as the area where I would meet with the whole group. It was often the only way I could be sure of having a blocks area large enough for even a few children to use without conflict. If you have lots of conflict in your blocks area, first make sure you have a surplus rather than a scarcity of space.

Large blocks are a wonderful thing for children to play with, but they can also be prohibitively expensive. Rather than have a few of the expensive kind that will last four generations, I suggest you buy many, many of the cheap cardboard kind you fold together yourself. One set currently costs somewhere under twenty dollars. I think two to three sets are a good amount if you have a blocks area that holds three children. In my experience, they last nearly as long as other kinds and don't hurt nearly as much if you accidentally get hit in the head with one! When children have enough blocks to build what they want, they can engage in negotiation over much more interesting things.

Classrooms often also have unit blocks in this area and the rule of surplus/scarcity holds. If you notice frequent arguments over how many blocks someone has, it may be that you have too many children playing for the amount of blocks. I have generally kept the unit blocks, when I've had them, separate from the larger building blocks. When they are on the other side of the area, for example, it seems like children are better able to work out logical space arrangements for themselves. It also helps to prevent problems caused by too many people trying to occupy the same space at clean-up time. Remember, it isn't that we don't want children to have conflicts, we just want to avoid the ones that have no good solution and that occur over and over again because of an ill-planned situation.

Because of the games we played with our former "doll corner," our blocks area included the following props: several baby-sized dolls, several animals and one stuffed carrot; assorted small pillows and blankets; a doll-sized cradle (the children loved the idea of climbing into it themselves—I always wished we could have one strong enough to hold them); a box containing about twenty diaphanous scarves; assorted trucks, cars, and small people; and a beautiful wooden ferry boat. Other things that we hauled in periodically included a large box full of plastic plumbing pipes and joints, a rocking boat that turns over into a bridge, two really large pillows (one of them had a blue slipcover and often became a pool to jump into), a case full of shiny belts, small road signs, large pieces of cardboard, and pieces of fabric. The variety of props helped to encourage a diverse kind of play.

Again, just as with dress-up, this area is an area where there will be many opportunities for increasing children's competence in negotiating. It is also an area that permits you to encourage new relationships between children by sometimes choosing the children to play there. It is rich in opportunities for cooperative problem-solving, building, and disassembling.

3.6 Table toys area

This area encompasses a great range of toys from puzzles to bristle blocks to playdough. I have found there to be two main issues of concern here: the quantity and kind of toy selected, and how to deal with the gun play that tends to develop when children are using small construction toys.

It is important to rotate the items available to children in this area, even if you have little extra equipment. "Retiring" a toy for a time always works to restore interest when it reappears. Another trick that has worked well for me has been to change the location of things and to casually put them out on the table to catch children's attention. New accessories for toys or placing them in a slightly different context can be helpful as well. Rather than limit our equipment to the standard items found in most classrooms, we often included anything that might be interesting as long as it was safe. Every once in a while, let your shelves house such things as a box full of buttons, a basket full of polished small rocks, a shallow tray filled with sand and small shells or small rocks and sticks, round glass pebbles in different colors used in crafts, assorted ceramic tiles, or anything else that looks like it might be fun to sort, arrange, and touch. Add a little something to your playdough by adding cut-up drinking straws or short lengths of colored telephone wire. Give those children who don't already know a chance to learn how to use chopsticks by putting out two pairs of child-size ones along with a pretty bowl containing small pieces of chopped-up sponge. One of the big favorites in our classroom came during a time when we were talking about personal ornamentation. We had collected a whole box full of old costume jewelry from among the parents and the children loved to go through it, sorting things and draping themselves. Often they liked to lay it out on the table and just look at it.

When purchasing more standard equipment, such as Legos, try to have plenty of one kind of toy to encourage cooperative play rather than parallel play with different toys. Rather than buy three different kinds, I have usually chosen to buy three times as much of one item. It seems to make a recognizable difference in the amount of anxiety children experience while waiting turns when they can foresee an early opportunity to play with that item. It is important to set a maximum number of children to use the toy in order to eliminate the struggle for an adequate number of pieces. You can set up the opportunity for cooperative problem-solving during clean-up by looking carefully at how things are stored. For example, if you have a lot of bristle blocks and a basket or section for each color, children will be able to work out ways to help each other get them all in the right place. It is a very nonthreatening way for them to experience working together to accomplish a task.

If you have enough room in a classroom, it is nice to have a project on which everyone can work that takes a while to do. I have often kept a "special" puzzle out for a week or two. I bought several inexpensive cardboard puzzles of 50 to 150 pieces and found that with a little encouragement—and some help!—from an adult, children will work together to complete the puzzle over several days. The puzzle remains out in a location near the door and does not get taken apart and put away at clean-up time or the end of the day.

Parents very often become involved in its progress, with staff encouragement, and will join with their child and other children in the effort to finish it. This technique has been very helpful in creating bonds between parents and other children in the class. The children are aware that this "special" puzzle is not one they are meant to be able to work alone. There are other variations on this theme such as giant constructions out of whatever you might have. I have used everything from small wooden blocks to colored plastic hair rollers and clips. (People bring me things . . .) You might also try making a right-angle corner out of mirror sections—be safe!—and build elaborate parquetry designs into the corner. The mirrors reflect it into a circular design and the result is fascinating to children and adults alike. Just remember to go over the rules with the children periodically, and clue the parents in too. People should not undo the work of someone else, but they may add what they wish. The result belongs to everyone and we should enjoy the changes.

One thing we frequently encounter in this area is that some children build guns or killer spaceships from small construction toys, then proceed to get involved in some violent play. Since we deal with the issue of violent play frequently and in a fairly positive way (please see the chapter, "Defining the Limits"), we do attempt to change the play. Generally, my intervention will take the form of discussing the issue with the child so that she has a clear understanding of the reasons behind the banning of killing games. It is important that this discussion is appropriate for the age level of the individual child. I then try to help the child find some other way she could play with that toy. If a child persists, I ask him to find another toy to use.

Another problem we had in the classroom was specifically with Legos and girls. We noticed at one time that the only children playing with them were boys. Girls were not touching them. We could not be sure why this was happening but we decided to try an experiment. First we removed the Legos from the shelf. This forced the boys who normally played with them all the time to find other toys. Then, during a part of the day when we did activities in small groups, we took a small group of children who normally did not play with them (boys and girls) and had a teacher work with them in the small group. After doing this on several occasions over a period of two weeks, we returned the Legos to the shelf. Most of the children who had been in the small group then chose the Legos on their own during some free-play periods. This strategy of taking the problem out of the free-play context and putting it in a controlled small-group setting also works well for other problems, such as exclusionary behavior, or two children who simply cannot work together without problems.

3.7 Free choice art area

This area can be a veritable whirlwind of creative and cooperative activity. It is important that it is a very "self-service" kind of area so that children can help themselves, help each other and put things away independently. In addition to the standard items such as scratch paper, crayons, markers, glue, and scissors, we tried to make sure we always had string and masking tape. Children love tape and most of them can easily handle 1/4"-masking tape on their own. The consumption of the precious tape went down to reasonable proportions after a time, when the children realized that it was usually there for the taking. Generally, it is best not to assume that more than two children can share a roll at a time. Encourage children to help each other with the tape rather than ask an adult. If need be, an adult can show them a way that two children can handle the job of cutting it or placing it.

Remember that children are much more likely to become involved in being cooperative when they share an interest and an excitement in what they are doing and aren't frustrated by a lack of material. I found that one of the things that helps to achieve this goal is to put out some kind of special material in a basket or other container. Some examples of materials might be colored paper strips, straws, paper muffin cups, old wrapping paper, cotton balls or anything else interesting that comes your way. Train any adults you know to bring you anything made of shiny paper or ribbons, small items of any quantity and anything they remotely think you might be able to use. Not all parents are happy to see it come home in the guise of "art," but the children have much to gain from making the conversion.

There is another way in which the idea of social responsibility can be made real in this area. Sometimes I would get my hands on limited quantities of very enticing materials, such as brightly colored feathers. It is tempting for some children to use great quantities and even attempt to hoard some. Rather than giving each child in the classroom two, take the time to sit down with a group of children and let them attempt to come up with some kind of solution. You may be surprised at the results. One time a group of children ended up choosing to have very few of one item so that another child could have all she wanted because it was important to her to make a thing that required many. This kind of process is the sort of activity that allows children to internalize the reasons for ethical and empathetic behavior.

3.8 Quiet area

In any classroom or home it is important for people to have a place where they can go to be by themselves, to work out a problem, or to be together with a special person in private. This is the function of the quiet area. The choice we made in setting up our quiet area was to make it large, comfortable, attractive, clean, and near the door. Ours had a rug, a large couch, two overstuffed chairs and a lot of pillows. We made every attempt to make it an attractive, calm place decorating it in shades of old rose. This need not be expensive at all. The area is used for reading stories to the group, as a place where one or more children can go lie down or sit together quietly, where a child who needs to be away from the group can be by herself looking at a book and as a place where children and adults can go to work out a problem. Parents like this area and will sometimes stop to read a story to some children before they go. This area also allows staff some opportunities to discuss things with a child in relative privacy and comfort.

Because this area is designated as a place for problem-solving and is at the same time a very relaxing spot, it helps to remove some of the tension from conflicts and facilitates their resolution. It is important to keep the uses of this area specific and not allow it to be used as a play area.

4
Defining the Limits

In the discussion of physical space and equipment, I talked about ways of arranging the *physical environment* to reduce conflict to manageable levels. Adults also have a considerable amount of power to arrange the *behavioral environment*. It's useful to think this issue through carefully, so we're conscious about the choices we make and are able to communicate them clearly to our children. If we arbitrarily rule out whole areas as unacceptable arenas for conflict and negotiation, not even acknowledging the possibility that another decision could be made, then we may easily leave children confused about the purpose of the skills we're trying to teach. ("I want you to learn conflict resolution skills, for use in the areas that I choose as appropriate. If you have a conflict with me about something I consider nonnegotiable, however, then you're out of luck.")

There are many reasons for setting limits in a child's environment. There are rules made to avoid danger, i.e., no jumping off the rafters. There are rules to prevent injury to other children, i.e., no throwing big wooden blocks at people. There are rules made to ensure the adults' good functioning, i.e., bedtime at 8:00 because I need some free time in order to stay sane; or, no sloppy paint projects because we can't stand the mess. There are rules made on the basis of adult value judgments, i.e., no physical conflict, no playing with food, no nudity, no profanity, no war play, no talking back. It's important to think our rules through carefully and acknowledge the different reasons behind them, so that children can see the choice-making process, and develop their own opinions about choices they might make.

4.1 One example: war play

Limits based in values are probably the most controversial—and one we set very firmly concerned war play. The discussion about children and toys that glamorize violence has gone on for a long time and seems destined to continue among parents and other early-childhood specialists for some time to come. Here is one woman's carefully considered and deeply held point of view.

a. Constraining the imagination

I feel that in looking at this issue it is important to keep in mind that what we are talking about are children in this society and in this time. A child who has grown up in a community at war has an entirely different experience and will have different needs. Children in the United States nowadays have a kind of war play presented to them that owes much of its character to television and marketing trends. It is the domination of this highly commercialized toy industry that makes it necessary to look even more closely than ever before at the impact it can have on children. The nature of the kind of toy marketing we find in toys like Transformers and the GI Joe series needs to be understood as a complicated phenomenon. The manner of the commercialization is one that through television's powerful imagery and rigid characterizations can easily cause restrictions in children's imaginative play. Even children who are not exposed to television programs, but rather have gained their information about a toy from other children tend to limit their play content to the "script" provided by the manufacturer. We need to be concerned about this lack of the child's input and what it says about the acceptability of simplistic solutions. I think that a number of these concerns are valid issues with other toys that are not of a violent nature, but are marketed in this manner. A good example of this kind of toy would be Barbies, whose marketing is aimed at girls, and which encourage rigid sex-role stereotyping. Of further concern with these toys is that careful examination of the stories reveals an implied sexism, racism, and intolerance of difference. Characters are often depicted in a rather flat and unemotional manner. I think we can do much better in providing children role models that validate their experience of the world.

b. The debate over war play

Not all violent play that occurs among children is based on particular toys, however, and we need to look at the place that violent play in general holds in the developmental lives of children. This kind of play is sometimes validated on the grounds that some specific developmental needs of the child are being met. I feel that there is some validity to this idea, but contend that in most cases those needs can be met in other more affirming ways. Let's look at some of the specific arguments in favor of war play. (I will use the term *war play* in a general sense to refer to play in which there is killing and other acted-out violence.)

"Children can gain mastery of impulse control by participating in war play." The development of impulse control has long been considered an important step in the development of the young child. By engaging in "pretend fighting" and assuming the roles of powerful fantasy characters, children are enabled to learn acceptable boundaries and maintain control over impulsive behavior.

It is true that one of the most difficult developmental tasks for many children is the ability to gain impulse control. It is, in fact, an issue that pervades their lives and the lives of their parents and teachers. Children's abilities to exercise this control and the attendant judgment vary greatly. For example, in a group of ten four-year-olds, there might be one who needs a fence in order to stay in a safe area, another who could stay on one side of a line drawn on the ground and another who could deal with "stay where I can see you." This same range exists in each child and is affected by what the child is experiencing at that moment. A child who is upset, excited, or totally immersed in play will have more difficulty with limits.

There are many things we can do with children to help them gain control over their impulses both in the context of play and of daily life. When children engage in war play they are likely to become very excited, and the play often escalates beyond the realm of their ability to exert control. This kind of play often culminates in hurt or angry children precisely for this reason. I think it gives children the experience of failing at impulse control much more often than it provides the experience of mastery.

"War play gives children the opportunity to understand the difference between real and pretend." Because this kind of play allows children to attempt roles which are very removed from their own reality—i.e., superheroes with super powers—it facilitates the development of an understanding of the difference between the real and the imagined.

It is a wonderful thing to see the imagination and creativity with which children approach life. There is so much good material available for parents and teachers to use with young children that doesn't involve violence and killing, there is simply no need to bring any material that glamorizes violence into their play. Telling the difference between fantasy and reality is just as valid if the child is being "Firebird" as it is as "Superman."

It also has been my experience that a greater sense of this ability to tell the difference is developed when we engage children in an active rather than a reactive role. Rather than having children be consumers of fantasy by just listening to stories which they can then integrate into their play, it is helpful to engage them in telling stories themselves.

"War play allows children the opportunity to try out a variety of roles." Through play, children can pretend to be people very different than they themselves are. The ability to act out these roles enables them to grow out of their primarily egocentric view of the world and understand the experience of other people. Role play allows children to sort through information about gender roles as well as deal with issues of good and bad.

This process of role play is important to the development of the young child and in talking about the discouragement of war play, we are not talking about the discouragement of all dramatic play.

What we are in fact talking about is thinking carefully about the quality of the material we are giving to children to take into this play. Wouldn't it be better to give them role models that are not stereotypically gender-bound or do not respond to all problems with force? Wouldn't it be better to give them role models that encourage them to think about other people and that have real strengths rather than just super powers? This approach doesn't have to restrict the imagination—who, after all, hasn't dreamed of flying?—but can include characteristics which affirm the potential in each of us.

"War play allows children to feel strong, powerful, and competent when acting out the part of the hero." Young children are often working on their own feelings as separate, competent people who can take care of themselves. They can experience feelings of competence and control through role play, ie., superheroes.

There are basically two issues involved in this idea. One of them has just been discussed and has to do with the quality of the role model. I want to give children a definition of strength that goes beyond the ability to smash things. For me, Harriet Tubman is a much better example of a strong person than Superman. Because they are in growing bodies children are very involved in their own increasing strength and they should be affirmed for it. I am very careful, however, to affirm children for different kinds of strengths as well. The idea that someone is not as good as someone else because they can't run as fast, or lift as much, or because they have some kind of disability is often the idea that underlies our celebration of physical strength. It has been my experience that this value sometimes gets communicated when we don't intend it to.

The other issue has to do with working on children's real feelings of competence and power. When children are treated with respect and made to feel comfortable about their rate of growth, they have less need to escape into characters who can rule others. Children can feel true competence and power in the ability to communicate well with others and in being able to solve one's own problems. War play not only does nothing to increase children's competence in this area, it can actually hinder this development due to the limited nature of the play.

"War play allows children to integrate information they receive about the world around them into their experience." Children do hear about war, soldiers, and crime, and because much of this information is frightening and difficult to understand they need to try and make sense out of it. They are fascinated by issues of life and death and need a way to integrate these ideas into their view of the world.

There is no way we can keep children shielded from the realities of the world which include death, violence, and oppression. As adults, we do owe them as much help as we can possibly give to deal with these frightening subjects. It is important to sense the limits of a child's understanding of these issues.

Materials that glamorize violence do not help to enhance, in the long run, children's feelings of security. Even though they tend to minimize the effects of killing (he's not really dead, he's just an actor), they also present a view of the world where violence is acceptable and occurs with frequency. Instead, adults should let children know that hurting and killing are serious things and that people have organized themselves in an effort to contain and prevent it. We need to let our children know we are all willing to be responsible in small and large ways to keep people from hurting each other.

It is irresponsible to give children a view of death that is gleeful and temporary when the likelihood that the experience of a death will touch their lives is great. The glamorization of violence removes all honesty from the presentation and leaves children confused when they have to face it themselves.

"War play allows children to express feelings of anger and frustration." For a long time it was believed that acting out violently was a cathartic experience for both adults and children and that this expression of angry feelings was essential for emotional well-being. The original proponents of this theory were Konrad Lorenz and Sigmund Freud, and even though current psychological theory holds this idea to be untrue, it is still frequently used to validate the usefulness of war play, stories of violence, and competitive sports.

Here's what Alfie Kohn, author of *No Contest*, has to say:

> There are few beliefs so widely held by the general public that have been so decisively refuted by the evidence. The catharsis theory by now has no leg to stand on . . .
>
> Watching others be aggressive does not discharge our own aggressiveness. What seems to happen instead is straightforward modeling: We *learn* to be aggressive. Our restraints against aggression are lowered. Whatever explanation we devise for this effect, however, one study after another has failed to show any catharsis effect . . .
>
> Third graders who were frustrated by experimenters did not become any less aggressive when they engaged in aggressive play afterward. (On the other hand, those children who had the frustrating behavior explained to them became significantly less aggressive.)
>
> Elementary school aged boys were more likely to shove or hit their peers if they had watched a boxing film . . .

Those social scientists who have reviewed or conducted the research on catharsis speak with one voice. "Innumerable studies of aggression in children have illustrated that attempts to reduce aggression through the use of aggressive and vigorous play therapy have the opposite effect . . . "[1]

In working with young children it is important that we validate their feelings and help them deal with them in positive ways. The following quote, which states this idea well, is from a book by Michael Schulman and Eva Mekler:

Contrary to some popular misconceptions, your child will not be doing damage to herself if she learns to keep her anger under control. Anger is not a gas that must be vented lest it do bodily or psychological harm. There is no evidence that choosing to deal with anger in a constructive rather than a violent way leads to ulcers or any other ill effects. True, stewing in one's anger may produce psychological distress (such as depression) or physiological damage (such as ulcers); but not because one hasn't cursed, screamed, or smashed someone in the face. It's not bottled up anger that causes problems; it's feeling helpless to change an enraging situation. Ironically, when we can find no remedy for our dilemma, ventilating our anger only confirms to us how helpless we are.[2]

Again I find myself returning to that one very simple idea. If we are honest when we deal with children, bestowing on them that wonderful fruit of respect—the truth, if we allow them to be honest with us and if we validate their feelings, if we give them the help they need to exert the maximum amount of control over themselves and their lives that a person their age can have, then they will be able to live quite well without playing at war.

This is just one example of a choice we've made for our environment. As we raise and educate our children, the power that we wield as adults will have an enormous impact on them. Knowing that we ultimately get to define the behavioral limits of their environment, it's important that we think carefully and well about different reasons for the limits we choose and the effect they will have on our children.

---

1. Alfie Kohn. *No Contest: The Case Against Competition*. Boston: Houghton Mifflin, 1986.
2. Michael Shulman and Eva Mekler. *Bringing Up a Moral Child*. Reading, MA: Addison Wesley, 1985.

II
Interacting with Children

In the last section we set up the environment to eliminate unmanageable levels of stress and to enhance feelings of acceptance and self-esteem. That is the setting. Now we bring in the actors. How can adults behave in this environment to be of most use to children?

Without question, one of the most important factors influencing the social and emotional development of young children in a program, classroom, or family is the demeanor of the significant adults in a child's life. There's that old saying with which we are all familiar: "Don't do as I do; do as I say." If asked, most of us would quickly reply we do not believe it is possible to train children in this manner, yet all too often we seemingly fall into the trap of behaving as though it worked. Children's ability to develop empathy, for example, is influenced greatly by the quality of their interaction with adults. There are specific ways we can tailor things we do with children to enhance their skills in this regard.

Just as it is important to take time to clarify our values, it is also important to take the time to speculate on whether our behavior and expectations of children are consistent with those stated values. I'll try to provide you with strategies for evaluating materials for your classroom, play-group, or home; for dealing with materials that glamorize violence, and for giving children play alternatives that stress cooperation.

I'll also talk about books. The way we use books and stories—how we choose them, how we read them, how we tell and write them—can also have significant influence on our children's understanding of themselves, others, and the conflicts they experience. Finally, I'll look at the basic skills in conflict resolution—developing empathy and understanding of consequence, communication, and negotiation. As we become more conscious of these skills as building blocks, we can notice how fully developed they are in any one child and take concrete steps to help that child move forward. Eventually, as the final part of the negotiation section shows, we can work our way out of the intervention role altogether, leaving competent, confident children to manage their own conflicts.

5
Alternative Adventure Play

We felt it was important to eliminate all toys and materials that glamorize violence from the classroom in order to avoid giving even tacit approval to such items. In addition, we decided we would intervene when instances of war play occurred and help children alter the nature of their play. It is important that children see adults as willing to take a stand on these issues. Sometimes adults are reluctant to set such limits, fearing they may somehow repress the child. If this limit is set in a positive, affirming way, there is no need to be concerned. It has always been interesting to me that quite a few people who have expressed reluctance about a "no-killing games" rule, have no such reluctance when it comes to forbidding swear words.

Once having made this decision, it became necessary to figure out where to draw the line. This can get pretty tricky, so it should be done together with other staff in a program and among all the adults in a household. Do you wish to include lunchboxes that have Transformers pictured on them? How about a child who is wearing a GI Joe T-shirt? In formulating guidelines, you need to take into account a realistic assessment of the means for enforcing limits, as well as other issues that may be involved for a family or parent. It is sometimes necessary to be flexible in your interpretation of guidelines.

For example, we had been doing pretty well in my classroom with compliance on this issue, when we started a new child late in the year. Peter was the world's cutest three-year-old (of course they all are!) and it pained me to see him come to school every day wearing an assortment of clothing virtually all of which featured He-man or Transformers or GI Joe logos. He was not oblivious to these clothes, rather was enthusiastically proud of them. I spent a few days validating and questioning with comments and questions like: "Wearing that shirt makes you feel good. What is it you like about it? Is that important?" At the end of that time I knew he was the youngest in a family of three children and that most of his clothes had always been hand-me-downs from his older brother. These clothes were also hand-me-downs, but from someone outside of the family. They were new to him and all his own! His mother was a single parent and had been on public assistance for a number of years. She was now working a difficult shift, making very little money, and needed the clothes given to her for the children. What was printed on the T-shirts was not of major concern for her, given the problems she had to face.

For me to approach this parent with a request that she discourage the wearing of these clothes would have been totally inappropriate and disrespectful. Taking away from this child's enthusiasm over his new clothes would have been cruel. By taking a long-range view, providing children with other positive role models, and by focusing on the personal aspects of Peter's pride that he had clothes that were "new" and his—the matter was handled in a positive, affirming manner.

Dealing with actual toys children bring to school can be somewhat easier. Some of the more common things children bring to school are toy weapons, small figurines (Star Wars, Superheroes, and Transformers, to name but a few . . .), as well as essentially "neutral" toys such as spaceships and construction toys. Anything which was a weapon did not get used in our classroom. It is important to talk to children frankly about the uses of guns and other weapons, and to explain that we as adults have strong feelings about hurting and killing. A good tool for organizing your thoughts and working out appropriate language for young children is "A Gun Is No Fun" in *Stories For Free Children* (Letty Cottin Pogrebin, 1982). Reading this directly to preschool aged children is probably not too helpful, as it is a little "old" for them. When a child brings such a toy to school, we ask the child to choose between sending it along with the parent or keeping it in their cubby. We allow as much time as required to explain to the child why it cannot be used in play in the classroom. It is also important to allow enough time for the child to tell you why that toy is important to them.

The figurine-type toys fall into a more ambiguous category. Children are not discouraged from bringing these items to school, but teachers carefully monitor their use. If the child uses the toy for playing fighting and killing games, we talk to the child and try to come up with some less violent suggestions for adventure play. It is important to assist the child in finding some alternative kinds of adventure play, rather than simply demanding that the game be changed. Should the child persist with the killing games, the child will be directed to another toy and asked to put that one away for a time. This approach creates opportunities for the discussion of several issues including the idea that what people *do* with things is often more important than the item itself. Something important to keep in mind should you notice you have this kind of play occurring persistently, is that children may not be receiving enough alternative adventure material.

You will also run into the problem of children using "neutral" toys, such as Legos, to create death-dealing spaceships and the like. As with figurines, discuss the inappropriate use, try to find an interesting substitute and, as a final resort, ask the child not to use the toy.

Always keep three things in mind:

1. Don't create a vacuum; you must help children find an interesting substitute for violent adventure play and satisfy their fascination with good and evil.
2. You must take the time to help children understand why you don't want them to play these kinds of games.
3. You must deal with any emotions the child may have at the time. Violent play does not always signal conflict in children, but you must be aware when it does.

Giving children alternative adventure material is really not as difficult as it sounds, and can be fun. There are many wonderful stories available in books you can seek out, but you can also create your own materials.

Although I don't consider myself a terrific storyteller, I have found children through the years to be very supportive and marvelously appreciative. I began making up stories in which children are the characters and they solve problems cooperatively and with kindness and empathy. Children like to hear the same stories over and over again, and adopt them freely as the basis for play. By asking children to participate in finding solutions to the problems stated in the story, we are often able to embark on some discussion of violent solutions and their efficacy. When telling one of these kinds of stories, I don't like to leave anyone out, so they are often populated by lots and lots of characters with bit parts. The children are usually very attentive when they know their name will occur in the story. And should I forget some detail and get it wrong, they're right there to correct me!

Because magic and imagination is important to many of us, I've also tried to find some other magical heroes to star in stories I tell. One of my favorites is the Firebird, inspired by a Harlem Dance Theater production of the Stravinsky ballet. I've made up a number of "Firebird" stories, and have been pleasantly surprised to find children playing games that involve her on the playground. A good source of inspiration for these kinds of characters is the storehouse of ethnic folktales available at most libraries. With folktales you must be selective. Many of them can be frightening or violent.

A third way of using stories that I have found both fun and productive is to make up stories that address a particular issue with which a child or group of children is struggling. The main character in these stories is always a child, but often not a real child in the class. If you use the name of a real child and their real problem, not only do you have to be very careful not to cause emotional damage, but you also need the child's permission to tell the story to others.

Your manner of helping children reconsider violent play will need to be very personal, and hopefully it will be propelled by your own sense of humor and adventure.

6
Books as Resources

If stories are a good way to help children deal with the great and small issues of life, then the books we read to and with children can be a wonderful resource. The impact of a favorite book on a child can be astonishing, and the collective impact of what we present to them in books conveys a great many values. It is for this reason that evaluating the books you use is well worth the time. I have one very simple rule: *Never use a book that you haven't read.*

A children's book conveys values in a number of ways. You should read the words and determine what the message of the plot is. For example, *Three Billy Goats Gruff* has a few dominant themes, but the main message is clearly that if you're big enough and tough enough, you'll be okay. There are many versions of this story and other ideas presented in it, but the conflict is always solved by an act of force. Sometimes it is difficult to pick out just what the message is, and sometimes an author will have attempted to give a different message than that which comes across. Because of this, we have had to let all staff have a try at it. We tape a small note soliciting comments to the book and let it make the rounds of all staff.

Books also convey values by their use of language. How many of the books in your local library still use the word *fireman* rather than *firefighter?* If you don't change the words when you read the stories, you will probably get more boys playing "fireman" in blocks than girls. Because we are all so used to this language, it is sometimes difficult for us to realize the impact it has on children.

Information presented visually has more impact than information that is heard. This fact makes it essential that we look at the values the pictures convey. Look carefully at the people presented in the book and at what they are doing.

When any of these three problems are present, the only one you can really change easily is a language problem. Although we had books of our own, much of our "rotating stock" came from the library. Because they were not ours, we couldn't just mark out words and put in new ones with permanent ink. For a time we settled on a more pro-social yet consciousness-raising strategy. We drew a line through the offensive word and wrote its replacement over it in pencil. Generally our changes were one word changes, increasing the number of female pronouns, for example, but sometimes we reconstructed a sentence. We always thought other people might actually appreciate the changes or that they might help others to think about the language . . . besides, it was erasable.

For a long time, we were actually supported in this venture by our friendly librarian. Eventually, she transferred elsewhere and her replacement requested that we find another way. We switched to little yellow "Post-it" notes which we could use in the books and then easily remove. Not marking these changes made it too difficult for staff to be consistent, and some of us had some difficulty reading the story with enough drama if we had to concentrate on the language that closely. The process of concentrating on a book's language also helps keep us aware of the language we use with children.

Another thing to bear in mind is the impact your whole collection of books makes. How many of the protagonists are strong females? How many of the characters are nonwhite? It can be difficult to achieve balance here, especially if you are dependent on the library for books. In practice, it sometimes means that you have fewer books available in order to achieve some kind of reasonable representation.

There is a lot of material that's wonderful and it's growing at a good rate. In selecting books, look for the following:

1. Books that depict a spectrum of ethnicities and other cultures with dignity and respect;
2. Books that show women, men, boys, and girls in nontraditional roles;
3. Books that deal with nonviolent means of resolving conflicts, and those which represent emotions and feelings in a positive and honest way.

The following questions may help to serve as a guideline for assessing books you use in your classroom or with your child:

—Are there any minority characters in the book?
—How are they portrayed?
—Does this book show a culture other than white, middle-class American?
—How does it show that culture? In a positive, respectful way?
—What gender are the characters?
—How are they portrayed? For example, are the girls and women essentially passive or are they shown as competent?
—Look at the dress of the characters. What does it tell you about them?
—What kinds of feelings do the characters have?
—What does the story tell you about those feelings? Are they good or bad to have?
—If there is a conflict, how is it handled?
—What is the value judgment presented?

—To what extent does the story represent a multiplicity of solutions? Does it imply only one possible solution to a problem?

—Are there things in the story which might be frightening or confusing to a child?

Because there really are so many good children's books available, it would be impossible to list them all. There is, however, a briefly annotated bibliography in the back of this book that lists a few books I've particularly liked.

Screening the books you or your children use can be somewhat overwhelming, and there are no hard and fast rules about it. It is a subject that begs for discussion, so we decided to have a "parent evening" where we attempted to tackle it. At the beginning, we were all in one group, and we presented parents with several books and asked them to comment. We had deliberately chosen one or two that we thought were awful, so the comments were interesting. We then asked the parents to break up into small groups of about four, gave them the above list of questions, along with ten books, and asked them to have fun. Staff circulated around and sat in on a group now and then, but that was primarily for our own interest. The parents had such a wonderful time that it was very difficult to get them to stop when we had run out of time. What we heard the next day was that many of them had come away with a new perspective on something they had previously taken for granted. We had many requests to repeat this particular kind of parent evening. As a classroom teacher, it was wonderful to have the parents be more aware of what we were doing. They finally understood what those little yellow pieces of paper stuck on the books were all about!

A final comment about books: Not only are books wonderful to read, but they are also wonderful to write as well. In our classroom, we frequently worked in small groups and made books. There was usually some kind of topic floating around the room, either something that had appeared in children's play, or something we had been focusing on in our activities. We didn't have a unit-based curriculum, rather we tended to have three or four "trains of thought" as the focus of our activities. On the following page is the text—too bad I can't include the pictures!—from a book called *Hair*, made while we explored different ways people ornament themselves.

"Hair.
It's for keeping us warm.
Without it we would be
bald as a scald.
Hair floats in water.

Hair protects us from bumps.
Barbers cut it.
Moms cut it.
Roommates cut it.

You can curl it,
put flowers in it,
make a bouquet in it,
braid it,
put it in a bun,
put it in a ponytail.

Hair.
It's good for us.

Elias's hair feels like a parrot and is the color of night and some trees.

Dane's hair is like a lion's and is light brown like Phoebe's friend's cat.

Phoebe's hair feels like a colt.
Its color is the same color as trees.
Very dark brown.

Leah's hair feels like a squirrel.
Colored like a tree, but more like a cat.

Nasim's hair feels like a bird.
The color of pale raisins."

—Leah Grupp-Williams, Elias Greendorfer, Nasim Simmons,
Dane Andrews, Phoebe Clark, and Nancy Redwine
(all between the ages of three and five, except Nancy)

7
Developing Empathy and an Understanding of Consequence

Our ultimate goal in working with children is to help them develop inner control and sensitivity to others. We want them to be able to choose actions understanding the consequences, and to have the tools to cope with those consequences. Part of being a human being is to act on impulse and to make mistakes. We need to give children the support they need to confront their mistakes and learn from them.

There are many opportunities throughout a day that expose children to the reality of intent, action, and consequence. Teachers must involve children in an examination of these events, so children can ultimately be empowered to make choices based on an understanding of consequence.

It was a bright, sunny day after three days of rain, and the children were glad to be able to play on the playground again. Kudra was making a big pile of wood chips, carefully scooping them up in his hands and carrying them to his "mountain." Andy and Joan were playing a chase game with each other, running around and squealing. Their game became progressively wilder and began to involve more territory. They were so intent on their game that they hardly noticed when Joan ran right through Kudra's "mountain," destroying it in the process. Kudra was angry and shouted at them, "Hey, you wrecked my mountain!" but they were so involved in their game they didn't hear him.

The teacher, who had watched this entire episode, called Andy and Joan to her. It took a few tries, due to the speed at which they were flying around the playground. They were annoyed at being kept from their game, and wanted to get back to it as soon as possible. She said to them, "I think Kudra has something he needs to tell you." Then she walked with them over to where Kudra was. He had, in the meantime, set about restoring his pile and was very involved in that task. When the teacher came over to him with the two other children and said, "Kudra, I think you had something you wanted to tell Joan," it took him a moment to think of what that might be. Then he remembered and said, "Joan, you ran right through my mountain and wrecked it!" Joan, anxious to get back to her game, said, "Sorry!" and turned to walk away.

At this point the teacher said, "Wait a minute. We have a little problem here," and gathered them into a little huddle. "How do you think it happened that you ran right through Kudra's pile?" she asked Joan. "I don't know," was Joan's response.

The teacher then turned to Kudra. "Kudra, can you tell Joan and Andy how you felt about having your mountain wrecked?" Kudra, who had returned to working on his pile said, "I didn't like it."

The teacher then turned to Joan and Andy, "Let's go over here and see if we can think of how you can keep it from happening again." All three went a small distance away from Kudra, who could continue his play undisturbed. The teacher then asked the two children, "What do you think the problem was?" Andy responded, "Joan wrecked Kudra's pile and he didn't like it." At this point Joan interjected, "Well, it wasn't all my fault, he was chasing me!" The teacher told Joan, "Tell Andy, and then let's see if you two can figure out what you need to change about your game to keep it from happening again."

The teacher waited patiently while the two of them worked through some ideas. When they turned back to her they suggested they could run in an area that had no other children in it. "Do you think you can remember to do that?" she asked them. They both responded affirmatively and then she told them, "I liked how you both worked that problem out together," and sent them back to play.

There are a number of other ways this teacher might have handled this situation. She might have ignored the situation, believing the children should work it out themselves. This would have required Kudra, the victim, to take the initiative and either go to the teacher to complain or chase down Andy and Joan himself. While we always want children to work through their problems as independently as possible, the fact that they ignored his initial remark indicates that he would remain unsuccessful.

The teacher might have taken the opposite position and restricted Andy and Joan's play without having the children engage in dialogue with each other. This would certainly solve the immediate problem for Kudra but would probably not do much to validate his feelings, or increase Andy and Joan's understanding of how their behavior impacted Kudra.

The intervention outlined in the anecdote achieves a number of things. Kudra gets an opportunity to state the problem to Andy and Joan in a setting where his right to express his feelings is validated. Andy and Joan get a very clear message that what another child has to say to them is important and that they have an obligation to listen. After Kudra has expressed his feelings, he is allowed to return to play and not held hostage to the efforts of the other children to find a solution. The teacher asks the children to define the problem and in so doing makes sure they understand that Kudra's feelings are the result of their actions. Sometimes this process can take a little extra time. The teacher then turns the problem over to Andy and Joan, making them responsible for figuring out what they need to change about their play. She remains at hand should they have difficulty and need help. She allows them to try out their solution rather than just eliminating the play. Should they continue to have difficulty, she can then go to them and say, "That was a good idea you had, but it doesn't seem to be working," and engage them in continued discussion.

Empathy occurs naturally in children, like a desire to explore their environment. Like curiosity, it varies from child to child and can be influenced by our responses to it.

A child's curiosity is enlivened when we respond patiently to a child's questions and when we ourselves ask questions intended to make her think about why something might be. In the same manner we strengthen a child's ability to respond empathetically in a number of ways.

The first thing to understand about "empathy training" is that it involves enabling the child to begin to make decisions about his behavior on the basis of the child's understanding of its consequences. An example of this kind of understanding is when a child doesn't throw a toy because she knows this will break the toy rather than because you have made a rule against toy throwing. The child who has this kind of understanding engages in a kind of internal dialogue and will tend to make decisions based on her own understanding rather than decide on the basis of whether or not she is likely to get caught. Learning about consequence requires that we explain about it to children and that they have opportunities to attempt predicting consequence.

We can take the story of Kudra, Andy, and Joan and look at how the teacher might have handled it had she chosen to intervene at an earlier point.

> Andy and Joan were playing a chase game that was growing increasingly intense, and they were covering an increasing amount of territory. The teacher noticed that Andy and Joan were so intent on their game that they were unlikely to notice Kudra who was building a mountain in one corner of the playground. She caught Andy and Joan and told them she wanted to talk to them for a minute. She said, "Your game looks like a lot of fun, but I notice that you aren't looking where you're running all the time. I think that might cause a problem. What do you think?"
>
> Joan responded, "I don't know."
>
> "Well, on that last time around the climber, I noticed that you came kind of close to Kudra over there. How do you think that is for him when you come by fast and close?"
>
> "It might be kind of scary," Andy volunteered.
>
> "Yeah, he might be afraid we would bonk into him," said Joan.
>
> "Mmmm . . . what do you think he would tell you about how that makes him feel?" asked the teacher.
>
> "Bad," was the answer from both children.
>
> "He looked kind of unhappy before," said Andy.
>
> The teacher responded, "Yeah, you can tell a lot about how people feel by what their faces look like, can't you? I'm glad you noticed that. Now, how do you think you can change your game so that Kudra can feel comfortable?"

In this case the adult didn't need to wait for the consequence to happen but chose instead to give the children an opportunity to try to predict what might happen if they didn't change the game. This particular kind of strategy is very useful. Even though we acknowledge that children do learn from mistakes, it's nice when children can learn without having to make a mistake. Predicting consequence gives children practice in analyzing a situation before a problem has occurred.

It is important to give children the reasons behind rules or give them the opportunity to try to figure out (in discussion) those reasons. Children who are not given reasons may or may not be obedient, but they will be unprepared to make good decisions about their behavior. We want children to make decisions about their actions in light of how that act will affect others as well as themselves.

It is important that the reasons we give children are specific and accurate as well as honest. Here are some examples:

> Randi took Patrick and Matthew to the park on a day when it had rained quite a bit earlier. Before she knew it, Patrick had managed to immerse himself in several puddles. Matthew, a bit more cautious, was still dry. She restrained Patrick and asked them both to stay out of puddles.
>
> Matthew wanted to know why he couldn't go in the puddle when Patrick had, and Patrick wanted to know why he couldn't any more since he was already wet.
>
> Randi explained that since they were staying at Patrick's house for the day, it would be possible to change Patrick's clothes on their return, but that she wished for Matthew to stay dry because she had no other clothes for him. She didn't think Matthew would feel very good if Patrick could go in the puddles and he (Matthew) couldn't. In addition, since they were both riding back in her car, she was hoping Patrick would dry out a bit so there wouldn't be quite as much mud on the seat.

In this case, Randi might have been tempted to say, "Because I said so." Patrick and Matthew had good questions and she needed to think to give them an honest answer that would be meaningful to them. She might have also been tempted to give them a more general answer like, " . . . Because it will make too much trouble for me." She, however, took the time to outline all the issues involved and give them very specific reasons.

> During story time the children came into the quiet area and sat on pillows or the couch. Although the space was comfortable, the children did sit closely together. Zenja ran into the area and jumped on the couch with her feet flying into the air. They almost connected with Sean's face. The teacher said, "Zenja, when you come in here and there are other people around, you need to walk in and sit down more calmly. When you jump like that your feet are very likely to hit someone and hurt them."

It was important that the teacher took the extra time to add the reason on to the request to Zenja. He knew that if he gave her the reason, she might be much more likely to think it through next time or the time after. He also gave her information that would allow her to understand why he might let her jump onto the couch at some other time when there were no other children around. In doing so, he gave her the ability to analyze the situation next time and make a decision on her own about whether or not she needed to slow down.

> Jon and Lena were very close friends and often inseparable during the day. Jon usually arrived at daycare earlier than she did and waited eagerly for her arrival. When she came in the door with her father, Jon ran to her, grabbed her, and hugged her with a great amount of energy. Lena's response to this was to cling to her father's leg and frown. After a few days of this, when it showed no signs of changing, the teacher decided to approach Jon about it. Rather than just tell Jon not to do it, she thought she would see if she could get him to figure it out. The next morning right after he had made his usual run for Lena, she took Jon aside.
>
> "You like Lena a whole lot, don't you?" she asked.
>
> Jon nodded.
>
> "It's probably pretty hard for you to wait for her to come to school sometimes, isn't it?"
>
> Jon nodded again.
>
> "When she finally comes, it seems like you want to run right over there and give her a big hug . . ."
>
> "Yeah, and I want her to come and play with me," answered Jon.
>
> "Have you noticed what she does when you do that?" asked the teacher.
>
> "Yeah," was Jon's reply. "She holds on to her dad and sometimes she even says mean things to me."
>
> "Why do you think that is?"
>
> "Maybe she doesn't want me to hug her?" questioned Jon.
>
> "I think you're right. Why do you think that is? It seems like she likes to give you lots of hugs at other times of the day," asked the teacher.
>
> Jon's reply was, "I don't know."
>
> The teacher decided it was time to explain. "Well, you know how when you first come in this room, sometimes you like to be alone with your mom for a little while? You like to take your time to say goodby and you want time to get a hug from her.
>
> Jon nodded.
>
> "I think maybe Lena wants to take some time like that with her father when she first gets here. I think that when you run over like that she may feel like you aren't giving her that time. I know that you're usually pretty anxious to see her, but do you think you could give her that time? I think that if you just keep playing when she comes in, she'll probably come right over to you when she's ready. Do you think you might like to try that tomorrow? I could help you if you want."

The teacher took the time to help Jon understand what Lena's response meant, and to validate his feelings. She then also took the time to help Jon understand Lena's response in a way that related it to an experience he'd had. The teacher followed up the conversation by approaching Lena when Jon was around, explaining that Jon would be trying this new thing on the next day, and asking Lena to let him know if she liked it. On the day following, the teacher helped Jon to remember. After Lena had finished sending her father out the door, the teacher engaged both of them in a conversation in which she encouraged Lena to tell Jon how she felt.

It is also important to give children an opportunity to understand that different people have different responses to a particular situation. What might feel good to one person may make another uncomfortable. This tolerance and understanding of individual response is important, and children learn it through discussions like these and from the kind of behavior adults model.

We also need to examine the role of intent. In the normal course of a day with a group of children, problems arise as a result of both deliberation and accident. If a child deliberately hurts another, we need to help them find some alternative expressions of emotion. When a child accidentally hurts another, it is still important that the children communicate. Many accidents among children are the result of not paying close attention. It is then important to help children understand that some change in their actions will help prevent such a thing in the future. Some accidents are unpreventable, and in that case it is important that both parties understand that it was a "no-fault" situation.

If this process sounds both time- and energy-consuming, that's because it is. It does not create instant compliance, but applied consistently, will ultimately enable children to work situations out by themselves to a greater degree. It will also work wonders on children's self-esteem and feeling of being in control of their lives.

In order for this process to work well, it helps if adults working together can agree that if one of them is engaged with children in one of these discussions, the other attempt to cover for him.

A vital point to keep in mind is that one of the most important ways children learn social skills is through modeling. If you model concern, honesty, respect, and thoughtfulness, you will make it possible for this kind of attitude to grow in the children in your care.

8
Clear Communication Skills

Of the skills needed for conflict resolution, the ability to communicate clearly is certainly one of the most important. There are a number of elements that make up clear communication leading to successful negotiation. Just because a child has demonstrated a good verbal ability does not mean she is able to practice clear communication. Communication skills can be broken down into two kinds: expressive and receptive. I'll deal with each of them separately, although both are essential.

8.1 Expressive communication skills

These refer to the child's ability to state her need clearly and can be broken down into some specific components.

a. Having the other person's attention

Children—and some adults!—have an amazing capacity to skip right over this detail. Remind children to check if the other person is listening or talking to someone else. Children need to address the other person by name and establish some eye contact with them. Please bear in mind that in some cultures direct eye contact is considered to be a sign of rudeness, so remain flexible if you think this may be the case with a child.

When interacting with children, it is important to remember to model this by getting down to their level, getting their attention before speaking to them and remaining focused on the child while speaking to them.

b. Being heard

Children need to speak in clear voices in the general direction of the other person. This can be difficult for some children and they need gentle encouragement while they learn.

c. Stating the problem clearly

This can be the most difficult part. We want children to be able to make statements that tell the other person what they need to do. Here are some examples:

"I won't be your friend anymore!" A more constructive option is: "I don't like it when you grab things from me. Please give it back."

"I *never* get to go on the swing!" A more constructive option is: "Would you let me have a turn on the swing please?"

"You're being mean!" A more constructive option is: "I don't want you to chase me."

Many of the activities in the third section of this book are designed to work on these skills, but the normal course of events provides many opportunities for practice. Clearly, modeling this sort of language for children in your interactions with them would be the first place to start.

The most useful sentence, and one that we used frequently, especially early in the year was:

"Tell me (him/her) what it is that you want (need)."

This was often the help that children needed to get on track, and it seemed that once a problem was stated in these terms, the solution was close at hand.

Interaction of an adult with a child often provides additional opportunities to get children into the habit of stating things in terms of what needs to be done. Here's an example:

> Child: "Hey, the pitcher is empty!"
> Adult: "Why, so it is. Is there something you'd like me to do?"
> Child: "Yeah. Would you get me some more milk please?"
> Adult: "Sure . . . be happy to."

These exchanges should always be friendly and may be inappropriate in moments of stress. In my experience, children tended to find them funny.

The same need for clarity is there when children are dealing with their feelings, especially anger. We've all heard children say things like, "You can't be my friend any more," or "You can't come to my birthday." In these instances, it is important that adults help children to state the problem and their feelings clearly.

An adult can approach children and, stating that she notices they have a problem, ask if they would like some help. She can say, "It sounds like Heather is angry about something. Do you know what it is?" The adult should encourage the children to talk to each other and restrict her role to helping the children state clearly to each other what they need. Again, in the initial stages of this work with young children, the adult may be required to model language.

8.2 Receptive communication skills

These are the other side of the coin. These entail listening and responding to what was said, remaining with the issue, and reading body language and facial expression.

a. Giving attention to the person who is communicating

Children may have difficulty focusing on the person who is talking to them. In such a situation, it is helpful to move children to a place where there are fewer distractions.

Children can also be highly skilled in the art of the "ignore," a tactic that can drive the person speaking to them into a frenzy. It is important to make it clear to children that if they are being ignored when they try to talk to someone, an adult will come and help them get that person's attention. It is important that adults take the time to follow through on that promise. The adult simply goes to the child and addressing the other states, "Benjamin has something he needs to tell you." He then lets the children take it from there to the extent they are able.

b. Remaining on the subject

Having children remain on track with their conversation essentially hinges on their continuing to state clearly what they need from the other person. Reassure children that there are several answers to a request, including "no," but give them an opportunity to come up with some other solutions for satisfying the needs of both parties.

c. Reading body language and facial expression

In addition to doing activities designed to foster an awareness of body language, adults may need to help children focus on the nonverbal communication of others. This can be done by gently encouraging children to look at another person and asking, "What do you think Larissa is feeling right now?"; "What does her face tell you?" When the child responds with either "She looks sad" (angry, etc.), or "I don't know," the adult should encourage the child to ask the other how they are feeling.

During the normal course of a day there may also be opportunities to comment on facial expression or body language that you see on other people. Observations like, "Boy, he sure looks angry, doesn't he?" and "Her face looks really sad. What do you think might be making her so sad?" can be helpful in getting children to attend to some of the nonverbal ways people communicate.

The common element running through all these specific skills is the ability of the child to focus on what's going on for the other person and to respond to it. Please bear in mind that everyone travels down this road at a different speed. These ideas should not be seen or presented in a context of right and wrong, rather they should be seen as a process of developing skill.

Some children may not be ready to participate in a conversation either as speaker or listener and should not be forced to do so. The adult can say, "I don't think you're ready to work on this problem right now. It needs to be solved, but you can have some time to think about it and tell Herman or me when you are ready to do so." If there is a toy in question, you may decide to hold it in "escrow" or to temporarily let another child use it until some agreement can be reached.

9
Negotiating Skills

Now that we've looked at the development of sensitivity to others, communication skills, and an understanding of causality, we're ready to talk about the payoff. Children can learn to negotiate their problems with each other.

As I said in the introduction, in order for children to engage repeatedly in constructive conflict resolution, the following needs to happen: The amount of conflict in your environment must be fairly low, so that the adult can guide the resolution process where necessary, so that the resolution process works for, and not against the child, thereby encouraging the child to use it again.

In any setting where there are young children and adults, it is inevitable that at some point there will be a conflict and the adult will become involved in it. The quality of the adult's intervention is important in allowing children to learn to solve problems.

9.1 Promotional interventions

Intervention can fall into one of two categories: the "adult-fix" category or the "promotion" category.

The "adult-fix" is any interaction in which the adult steps in and creates a solution. It can range from the very simple and essentially dictatorial—"If you kids can't play without fighting, then you can't have that toy"—to a more complicated intervention in which the adult may be attempting to create a fair solution—"Juanita had it first, so you have to give it back to her." These interventions are generally marked by judgmental comments, finding fault, and a solution that comes from the adult and is imposed on the children. In our experience, this kind of intervention usually results in the cessation of the play between the children.

In the "promotion" approach, the adult's intervention is as limited as possible, and exists solely to promote problem-solving between children. The adult is there to encourage communication between children, to encourage input from children, and to keep children focused on getting to a resolution. The outcome of this kind of intervention is usually a continuation of the play between children. This process takes a lot longer and requires both patience and restraint on the part of the adult, but is worthwhile in the long run.

Children can engage in conflict resolution and will do so with enthusiasm. But it is necessary for adults to provide the practice and the tools for doing so. In observing this process in our classroom, we broke down children's varying abilities into three skill levels. Each of these skill levels requires a particular kind of teacher response. Remember that not only will each individual be at a different level, any pair of children in a conflict situation will be at a certain level as well. Your intervention needs to be guided by the ability of the pair.

Regardless of the skill level, the problem-solving will proceed along the following steps:

1. Calming and focusing
2. Turning attention to the parties concerned
3. Clarification/stating the problem
4. Bargaining/resolution/reconciliation
5. Prevention
6. Affirmation

I think the best way to understand the different adult roles is to illustrate the three levels with a similar problem.

a. Level I: High adult intervention

At this level the adult is very involved in problem-solving, helping to define the problem and modeling language.

Maria is doing a puzzle. Sean comes over and takes a puzzle piece from the ones on the table, reaches over Maria's arm and tries to fit it in the puzzle.

The teacher is alerted to the situation by both children screaming as each has a hand on a puzzle piece and is struggling to take it away from the other.

Knowing these children will not be able to resolve this problem without help, she moves over to where they are and kneels down to talk to them. Calmly she says, "Excuse me, would you hand me the piece please?"

The children let go of the puzzle piece, but both begin to talk to her, upset, and with loud voices. She gently touches both of them and states, "Wait, wait. You'll both have a turn to talk. Let's all take a deep breath and be quiet for a minute." (*focusing and calming*)

"Now . . . (she turns to Sean) I'm going to ask Maria to talk first, but you're going to have your turn too. It will help me a lot if you don't interrupt her." She then turns to Maria and asks, "Would you tell me what the problem is?"

Maria begins to explain while the teacher listens. Sean interrupts on several occasions and the teacher reassures him that he will have a turn to talk, then goes back to listening to Maria. Then Sean is given an opportunity to explain the problem. *(attention to parties concerned)*

During this exchange the adult should just listen—the problem will become clear in the explanations the children give. What is important here is that each person have an opportunity to tell his story. The other child, by being placed on hold, will inadvertently hear the other child's perspective. When the adult has heard both sides, she then states the problem in clear and simple terms.

She says, "So, the problem is that Maria didn't like it when Sean took the puzzle piece from the puzzle she was working, right? And Sean wanted to help Maria work the puzzle. Is that right?"*(clarification)*

Now she is going to help them talk to each other. She turns to Sean and says, "Tell Maria what you want."

If Sean doesn't come up with the language himself, the adult should model. "Tell her that you want to help her with the puzzle" or "Why don't you ask her if she would like some help with the puzzle?"

Maria may not want any help; she may merely make a face at the prospect and say nothing in reply. Again the adult should model language: "Tell him that you don't want any help right now."

Maria turns to Sean and says, "I don't want any help right now." Sean responds, "Okay, I'll get my own puzzle." *(resolution)*

The teacher needs to support Maria in her decision to work alone, but can help Sean to find an alternative choice of play if necessary. After going through a discussion like this, the most the adult needs to say about the initial grabbing might be a comment like, "It's usually a good idea to ask people if they want help." *(prevention)*

To close out this interaction, the adult can take a moment to praise the children for their part in resolving the problem. "I think you did a good job talking to each other (not interrupting each other, listening to each other, etc.)" *(affirmation)*

Children do seem to have a great interest in learning these skills and will often engage in practice during play. One of my favorite incidents took place on the playground.

Shilpi and Leah were inseparable friends and spent most of the day together. They both had a tendency to reach for things quickly and without asking. As a result, they had both needed the help of staff to work out their problems on several occasions. On the playground, they were involved in playing some sort of game together. When another teacher came to me and said "You've got to watch this," I paid a little closer attention to the content of their game.

They reversed roles every other time, but the script remained unchanged. Shilpi pretended to play with a doll and Leah walked over and pretended to grab the doll, at which point Shilpi pretended to hit her. Leah pretended to cry and said, "I don't like it when you hit me!" Shilpi responded with, "And I don't like it when you grab my doll!" They then paused for a moment and Leah said, "I'm sorry. Can I have a turn with the doll?" Shilpi then responded with, "I'm sorry I hit you," and gave her a hug. Then one or the other said, "I know! Let's both play with the doll together," and they ran off hand in hand. Then they walked back, switched roles, and started the whole thing all over.

They played this game often over a period of weeks and eventually had fewer problems with each other during their other play.

b. Level II: Minimal adult role

At this level, children define the problem using their own language and the adult merely clarifies when needed.

Maria is doing a puzzle. Sean comes over and takes a puzzle piece from the ones on the table, reaches over Maria's arm and tries to fit it into the puzzle.

Maria turns to Sean and says, "I'm doing this puzzle."

Sean answers, "Yeah, but I know where this piece goes."

Maria responds, "No!" and begins to push Sean's hand away from the puzzle.

Sean continues to try to fit the piece into the puzzle. The teacher, having watched this for a while to see how it would develop, comes over. She speaks to both of them. "It looks like you have a problem. Would you like some help?" (Because these children are not really agitated, her statement is sufficient for *calming*)

Maria speaks to the teacher, "Yeah, he won't give me back my puzzle piece."

The teacher says to Maria, "Tell him what you want." (*attention to parties concerned*)

Maria then turns to Sean and says, "I want you to give me back the puzzle piece." (*clarification*)

At this point, the adult needs to make sure Maria has Sean's attention and is speaking to him in a voice he can hear.

"But I just wanted to help her do the puzzle," he responds to the teacher.

She says, "Tell her what you were doing and ask her if she would like some help."

When Sean does that, Maria answers him with, "But I don't want any help. You can do the puzzle after I'm done." (*resolution*)

In this interaction, the adult models language and clarifies only as needed. It is important to remember that your objective is to get the children to talk to each other. When an adult is present, their tendency is to address their concerns to the adult rather than to the other child. With children at this level, the adult should attempt to leave the situation at the earliest point possible.

We developed an interesting tool to use with children at this level. The impulse to interrupt was very strong, in adults as well as children, and we felt this interfered with listening. Rather than listening, the other person tended to get invested in what they were going to say and listened for a place to interrupt rather than for content.

We made something we called "talking sticks." These were 3/4 inch dowels, about five inches long, which we covered in glitter. Any discussion used one stick no matter how many participants. The person holding the stick had the floor and could not be interrupted. When they were finished they handed the stick to another person, who then had the opportunity to speak. Because a person couldn't ask for the stick, but rather had to wait until it was handed to them, it seemed like the speaker was more relaxed and the listener more attentive to content. Some of the people who had the greatest difficulty were the adults!

We needed to train children in the use of the talking stick, first by explaining and then using it in a group format. We made a circle where everyone had a turn to answer a question, and children handed the stick from one to the other. It is important that the children themselves do the handing. There are children for whom it is difficult to let go, but with time they get much better at it. After doing that for a time, it was possible to use it in actual problem situations with small prompts from the adult. As the adult, it is important to play by the same rules and wait to be given the stick. In my experience, children tended to give it to the adult when they knew the conversation was not constructive. In time, children went to get the sticks on their own when they had a problem.

I think this works because children always do better when they have a concrete token for an idea. Many children took this idea home with them and continued to use it. My favorite story is one that a former Willows parent told me. One day both parents became involved in a discussion that grew increasingly heated. As feelings rose higher, there was less and less listening and more and more talking. After listening for a while, the child left the room, got a stick from his room—we gave them to children to take home—and handed it to his parents and explained the rules. They were amazed and realized that their child had demonstrated a wisdom beyond their own.

c. Level III: Children Taking Charge

At this level, children can go off by themselves to solve the problem. In my classroom, they grabbed a stick and headed off for the couch. They were usually smiling. The transition from Level II is achieved by the adult beginning to suggest to the children that they could go solve the problem themselves. The adult should assure children that their play spot will be saved and that they are free to come and get help if they need it. I always liked to have the children come back to me and tell me their solution so I could check to make sure it was mutually satisfying. It also gave me an opportunity to praise them for their ability to solve problems and I always liked to hear the novel solutions they came up with.

Maria is doing a puzzle. Sean comes over and takes a puzzle piece from the ones on the table, reaches over Maria's arm and tries to fit it into the puzzle.

Maria tells Sean, "I'm doing this puzzle!"

Sean responds, "Yeah, but I know where this piece goes."

Maria says, "No!"

The teacher has been observing and judges that they will not take the initiative to remove themselves from the table to work this out. She goes to them and suggests, "It looks like you two are having a problem. Would you like me to save your place while you go to the couch to work it out?"

The children go to the couch and return shortly.

Maria tells the teacher, "We've decided I'm going to do the puzzle alone and then we're going to do one together."

The teacher asks Sean, "Is that okay with you?"

Sean nods and she tells them both, "I'll bet it felt pretty good to work that out all by yourselves. Good job!"

You should be just as aware of each child's skill level in negotiating as you are of other developmental areas like gross and fine motor skills. Do not underestimate the children's ability to engage in this kind of negotiation, but also be flexible in your expectations of a child who may be having a difficult day.

Sometimes the most difficult part of helping children negotiate is resisting jumping in when the "perfect" solution seems obvious. Remember that even though it may seem perfect to you—it is *your* solution. Sometimes the process of resolving a situation does not go as smoothly as illustrated in the examples, particularly when children are moving from one skill level to another, or having a stressful day.

Negotiation learning in children is a prime example of the importance of process over product. Please remember that children must have the freedom to agree or disagree. That means that sometimes there simply will be no solution that suits both parties 100 percent. Life is like that, and your job is then to help children cope with their feelings about it.

III
Activities

Objectives

The activities listed in this section are each designed to meet several of the objectives explained below. Many of the activities will also meet other educational objectives, but I have not listed these, as they fall outside of the scope of this book.

These activities come from a vast number of sources. Some of them were invented by myself or staff with whom I've worked. I have attempted to give credit when I know the source. Some are ideas that have been adapted from other sources. They exist in that pool of ideas that people who work with children share. In no case has it been my intention to steal an idea without giving proper credit.

1. Cooperative task completion This includes cooperation both within and between groups. We avoid competition between groups, instead try to set up a situation where cooperation *between* groups is the outcome. Another aspect of this objective is the group's cooperative response to the choice of an individual. This idea appears several times throughout this list of objectives.

2. Improve communication skills This involves both expressive and receptive communication skills as discussed in Chapter 8, "Clear Communication Skills." We want to expose children to recognition of and respect for an individual's choice. We also want children to experience cooperative and supportive response to individual choice.

3. Body awareness Here, we are interested in fostering the children's awareness of their own bodies and the bodies of others. An important aspect of this category is the confirmation of the body rights of the individual.

4. Self-esteem/affirmation Activities in this category are meant both to affirm children and to allow them to affirm each other, including the physical expression of affection. We want to reinforce the special value of each person and those with whom they live.

5. Foster altruistic behavior Activities should help children develop empathy through increased understanding of others' feelings, and promote a breakdown of distrust.

6. Analogy and consensus We can provide children with the experience of reaching consensus in the controlled setting of an activity group. It is likely that children will be able to generalize this experience to their own interactions with each other.

In addition, we can provide them with a structured activity group in which the task is analogous to an experience in which the constructive cooperation is required. At least two people must sing together in order for harmony to occur.

7. Preliminary activity These activities work to establish basic skills or a structure necessary to do a more complex activity.

8. Fun I won't list this one on each activity. Every activity has been tested for fun by The Willows kids and staff. We always figured that those with whom you can share laughter become a small part of you.

General guidelines

—Make sure children who may not wish to participate have a place from which to observe. Respect any child's right not to participate.

—These activities are meant to foster an increasing and understanding of *nonverbal* communication, in addition to other objectives.

—Many of the activities are sequenced. It may not be necessary for your group to begin with the simplest.

—Remember that your personal teaching style must dictate your presentation of the activity, so be true to yourself.

Dictated Drawing

Number of children: 2-6 (children work in pairs)

Objectives:
1. Cooperative task completion
2. Improve communication skills
3. Body awareness

Materials: Felt pens or crayons, paper (common bond paper will do)

Procedure: Sit at a table with children paired. Give each pair of children the task of producing a picture of some sort. Explain that this can be a design rather than a picture of an object.

One child should do *all* the drawing, but *only* at the *verbal* direction of their partner. The person drawing may ask questions to clarify the instructions given to them. The role of the adult is to help children formulate the questions and directions. (I.e., what color, what shape, what size, above, below, next to?) The adult must also help keep the "draw-er" from making decisions on their own.

It is a good idea to explain to children that while they should give instruction to their partner, they should *not* criticize the other's work. Encourage children to observe the body language and facial expression of their partner to help them be aware of the comfort of the partner. Leave enough time to repeat with roles switched.

Comments: I advise children in the beginning stages of this activity to draw a design in order to avoid situations where a child may be dissatisfied with the quality of the picture drawn by their partner.

This can be a difficult activity and we do not advise it on a high-energy day, or if you, the adult, feel stressed.

We have found a noticeable increase in children's ability to work together and communicate, and we do this activity frequently. It is also an excellent way to work with two children who may have special problems getting along with each other. Quite often children will continue this activity after the adult has left.

Remote Control Drawing

Number of children: 1-6 (children work in pairs)

Objectives:
1. Cooperative task completion
2. Improve communication skills
3. Body awareness

Materials: Felt pens or crayons, paper (a common bond paper will do)

Procedure: Sit at a table with children paired. The number of pairs you work with should be determined by your ability to remain calm and guide the children with *pleasurable* success. Each pair of children draws a picture or design. One person holds the pen, but is otherwise passive. The second child moves the hand of the first child with their hand. Encourage children to observe the body language, facial expression, and verbal cues of their partner to help them be aware of the comport of their partner. Repeat this activity with the roles reversed.

Comments: Generally, this activity works better if children have had several opportunities to try "Dictated Drawing."

This can be a difficult activity and we do not advise it on a high-energy day, or if you, the adult, feel stressed. It is, however, immensely valuable in getting children more in touch with each other.

I'm All Torn Up
Thanks to Cheryl Nelson for this idea

Number of children: 1-15

Objectives:
1. Improve communication skills
2. Self-esteem/affirmation
3. Altruistic behavior/empathy

Procedure: You are going to tell the children a story:

"I'm going to draw a picture of (fill in a name)." (Do so, explaining what you are doing while you draw a full figure drawing of a person.) "_____ woke up this morning feeling happy. She was anxious to get to school and play with all her friends. Yesterday, the teacher had promised her a turn on the new toy and she was looking forward to it. She got dressed and skipped downstairs to have breakfast. When she got downstairs, the first thing her father said to her was, 'Oh! Those pants are filthy. Go and put on a clean pair . . . and hurry, or we will be late!' _____ did not feel quite as good anymore." (At this point tear off a piece of the picture and put it down beside you.)

"When she came back downstairs she tried to drink her milk quickly so they wouldn't be late, and it accidentally spilled. Her father said, 'Oh! Why don't you watch what you're doing?' She felt a little less good after that." (Tear off another piece of the picture.)

"When they were in the car going to school, _____'s brother poked her with a book. When she complained, her father said, 'Please be quiet. I hate it when you fight all the time.' She felt a little less good." (Tear another piece).

"When they got to school, the teacher was busy and only said, 'Hello' before she went to help someone else. She felt less good." (You got it—tear another piece.)

"Her father was in a hurry and left without giving her a kiss. She felt even less good.

"Two of her friends, Amy and Paul, were playing with a doll Paul had brought from home. When she asked if she could play with them, Paul said, 'No, I only want to play with Amy.' She felt less good.

"She went and asked the teacher if she could have her turn to play with the new toy, but the teacher told her she couldn't because it was almost time to clean up. She felt even less good."

(You may add some more instances, or change them to reflect some things that have actually happened to a child that day.)

"By that time _____ wasn't feeling very happy any more."

Ask and discuss: How was she feeling? Have you ever felt this way? Why? Let's see if you can think of some ways _____ could feel better. Discuss the things the child could do herself to feel better and some interactions with others that could do the same. With each good suggestion, allow a child to help you tape a piece back on the picture until it is whole again.

Comments: This is an activity that can be used with one child who is having a bad day, and can also be useful on "one of those days." I suggest it also be used on days when children and teachers are feeling good.

In a family this can be a very useful tool for talking about a bad day with a child. Allow the child to tell you the unpleasant instances.

Tangled Raisins
Thanks to Renee Motley for this idea

Number of children: 5-10

Objectives:
1. Cooperative task completion
2. Improve communications skills
3. Body awareness
4. Analogy and consensus

Materials: Small boxes of raisins or other treats (one per child), 20-foot lengths of string or ribbon (one per box)

Procedure: Tie the string around the boxes of raisins, then hide the raisins and run the string around the space you are using. Do this with each of the boxes, tangling the string in the process. Each child is given the end of one string and must find their way to the attached box.

This game also works if the children work in pairs. Do not underestimate their ability to *quickly* untangle the strings!

Comments: You may wish to let the children do the task, then have a discussion afterwards about some ways that worked better than others. If, however, you have a large group of children who are not in the habit of cooperation, you may wish to have some discussion prior to starting and make the group small.

This is an excellent party game!

Cooperative Spider Web

Number of children: 5-10

Objectives:

1. Cooperative task completion
2. Analogy and consensus

Materials: Ball of string, area large enough for children to sit in a circle

Procedure: Explain to children that you are going to make a giant spider web, but that this will only work if everyone does their job. Have children sit in a circle. The circle should be fairly small so children can roll the ball of string to each other.

Start with one child, handing him the end of the string and the ball. He should use one hand to hang onto the end and the other hand to hold the ball.

This child then rolls the ball to another child in the circle, who also holds onto the string with one hand while rolling the ball to another child. Continue in this manner.

You may have to remind children frequently to hold on, because if everyone doesn't hold on to the string the entire web will collapse. Don't worry if children occasionally roll the ball to the person sitting next to them. Continued movement of the string will ultimately result in a web.

Comments: The first few times, the adult may wish to remain outside of the circle in order to help children continue to hold and/or to help the ball of yarn reach its destination.

It is sometimes possible to have a discussion of some real life instances in which everyone must do their part or things don't work well.

I've found that a heavier string works better than a very thin one.

Body Sculpture

Number of children: 5-18

Objectives:
1. Cooperative task completion
2. Improve communication skills
3. Body awareness
4. Self-esteem/affirmation

Materials: None

Procedure: In a large group, all children sit in a circle or in a small group, in comfortable spots where all can see. Generally, it is best if the adult has the first turn in order to demonstrate the activity.

Select a child who is willing to have you turn them into a sculpture. Remember that children have the right to refuse participation. Tell the child she needs to freeze in the position into which you place her. Move the child's arms and legs gently into position without verbal direction. Make it clear to the child who is being molded that she should tell you if a position is uncomfortable for her. When you have finished, indicate this to the group and encourage them to applaud your efforts.

The child who was the statue should then ask another child to be her statue and proceed. For more interest, you may have the "sculptor" use more than one child in a composition. Discuss the gentle movement of the sculptor and the relative comfort or discomfort of the "sculptee."

Comments: This is also a good party game and could also be a fun activity for a parent/child evening.

We have added new interest to this game by incorporating large loops of elastic band and colored scarves into the sculpture. Use your imagination!

Shapes and Lines Collage

Number of children: 2-6 (children work in pairs)

Objectives:
1. Cooperative task completion
2. Improve communication skills

Materials: Construction paper, some cut into shapes and thin strips, paste, paste brushes

Procedure: Children work in teams of two. One child is the director and tells the second child what he wants the other to glue down and where on the paper to place it. The rule is that the child who is gluing must do what he is told by the other child and the child who is telling must make sure the other child understands. The idea is for children to communicate with each other when the directions are unclear.

When one design has been finished, have the children trade roles. Upon completion, ask them which role they preferred and why.

Comments: This activity can be very useful for helping two children who may not otherwise be getting along. It can help them develop some new habits for dealing with each other.

When dealing with children whose descriptive language skills are not yet well developed, I've found it constructive to limit the sizes and colors of the shapes used in the activity.

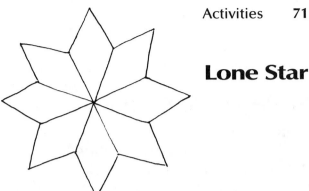

Lone Star

Number of children: Up to 10

Objectives:
1. Cooperative task completion
2. Improve communication skills
3. Analogy and consensus

Materials: Finished sample pattern, base paper (with pattern drawn on it if needed), diamond shapes cut out of colored paper, glue

Procedure: The name of this pattern is "lone star" and it is a traditional quilt pattern made from elongated diamond shapes. It is interesting to do this activity utilizing any number of traditional quilt patterns.

Children can work in pairs or trios. Show them the completed pattern. Essentially, each team has the job of figuring out how to put together the "puzzle" of the pattern with the colored paper shapes. Encourage children to figure out how to put it together before they begin to glue. This can be a difficult task, and in assessing the skill level of the children with whom you are working, you may decide on a more simple pattern. Remember, though, in order for children to engage in cooperative problem-solving, the task must have sufficient challenge to *be* a problem. Please remember also that this should in no way be construed as an art activity since it has nothing to do with creative expression. It is a problem-solving activity.

The role of the adult is to facilitate communication, have children reach consensus, and help the team figure out how to complete the task.

Comments: Any other parquetry or quilt pattern will work as well, although they differ in skill required. This activity can be done by presenting children with increasingly complex patterns as children develop their skills. This could also be an interesting way to use tangrams.

As an extension you can have a set of parquetry blocks available elsewhere in the room so that children can continue their collaborative work with them.

Group People I

Number of children: Up to 12 (children work paired or in groups of three)

Objectives:
1. Cooperative task completion
2. Improve communication skills
3. Body awareness
4. Analogy and consensus

Materials: Magazine cut-outs of legs, torsos, arms, heads, etc. (try to use pictures that present some alternatives to the standard white fashion models), glue, and paper for base

Procedure: Have the collage pieces ready prior to the time of the activity. This allows you to ensure that the variety of people shown is multiethnic and nonstereotypical It also allows young children to immediately engage in the task at hand, without having to struggle through the task of finding pictures to cut out. If the body parts are already separated and in sufficient quantity, children will not be tempted merely to replicate the original photograph. This activity could also be done using the body parts of animals.

Tell children they will have an opportunity to put together pictures of people from the separate parts available to them. Encourage them to use their sense of humor in doing this task. The first few times children are working together they should work in pairs rather than trios, as the dynamics of the situation are better for producing clear communication and consensus.

Comments: The role of the adult in this activity is to direct communication and elicit explanations from children as to why they have chosen to put the person together the way they have.

Group People II

Number of children: Up to 10

Objectives:
1. Cooperative task completion
2. Improve communication skills
3. Body awareness
4. Analogy and consensus

Materials: Crayons or markers, paper, scissors, glue

Procedure: Tell a story about a character in which you name the character but offer no further physical description. Then tell children you want them to make a picture of this character.

Pair the children off (later they can work in trios) and assign a body section to each pair (i.e., head, torso, arms, legs, etc.). The number of children with whom you are working will dictate the divisions of the body. It is best to have a large sheet of paper on which you will eventually mount the parts and put the character together. Advise children that their work will have to fit on this sheet. The size can be controlled by the size of the paper you give them. My advice is: go for large!

When all teams have finished, work together as a group to mount all the parts of the character and have the children explain their work.

Comments: The role of the adult is to aid in communication, helping children to reach agreement and spurring children on to greater graphic complexity by questioning.

Walk in the Dark

Number of children: 3-8

Objectives:
1. Cooperative task completion
2. Body awareness
3. Foster altruistic behavior

Materials: Flashlight, dark room

Procedure: Tell children you will take a special walk through the room. Remind children about taking care with each other and staying with you. Make the room as dark as possible, keeping an eye out for any child who might be frightened, then ask children to follow you and explore the room with the flashlight. Let your only limits be dictated by safety—go under tables, into corners, have fun!

This activity might well be done in pairs also.

Questions to ask: How do things look different? Is the color the same? Are the animals behaving differently? Would you like it if it was dark all the time?

This is a good opportunity to talk about feelings children may have around the issue of darkness.

Comments: One variation is to have a flashlight day, when each child brings a flashlight, and everybody explores on their own. As an ending you can have a "flashlight dance" in which all lie on the floor on their backs and let the lights "dance" on the ceiling.

Favorite Things Chart

Number of children: 5-8

Objectives:
1. Improve communication skills
2. Self-esteem/affirmation
3. Foster altruistic behavior

Materials: Lined paper, markers

Procedure: Choose your day and mood carefully so that you are not boring! On a large sheet of paper, mounted so that all the children can see, make a space for each child. One at a time, ask children what their favorite color is and then write that child's name in that color marker in the space provided. From there on, ask children to name some of their other favorites. You can no doubt think of lots of different questions to ask. The following should serve as examples:

—What's your favorite food?
—toy?
—song?
—thing to drink?
—animal?
—plant?
—time of day?

Drawing simple pictures next to the word can be helpful for children.

Involve yourself as much as you can in this discussion, encouraging children to think through the reasons for their choices. As the conversation progresses, point out differences and similarities.

Do not be overly concerned about children who have no original comment of their own and who copy the answers of other children. For some reason, these children do not feel safe articulating their own choice in this situation and you should be accepting of that.

Comments: This activity can be pursued repeatedly throughout the year and with new children. It is important to have children feel that their choices are important, so do not attempt to work with too large a group.

Make it clear that making fun of another person or commenting negatively on their choice is definitely not okay.

You can also leave the chart up with a space for parents and children to fill in about parents' favorites or their child's favorites when they were a baby. This is a nice way to involve parents.

Partner Circle Aim

Number of children: 4-6

Objectives:
1. Cooperative task completion
2. Improve communication skills
3. Body awareness

Materials: Paper with large circle drawn on it (several), markers or pencils, blindfold

Procedure: Children should be paired in teams of two. Even though I use the word team, they are not in competition with each other. This activity works best with older children who understand the terms "up," "down," and "to the side." It also requires children who are comfortable with the idea of being blindfolded. Sometimes a paper bag over the head is more comfortable for children than a blindfold. Working with more than three teams is too difficult and stressful for the adult, so I discourage it.

The aim is for the blindfolded person to make a mark inside the circle. There are two variations of this game:

1. The guide uses touch to move the "draw-er's" hand in toward the circle. A more sophisticated version of this would be to draw a road on the paper for the pair to work on.
2. The guide verbally directs the "draw-er."

Comments: This should be repeated frequently; increasing skill comes with practice. We sometimes have found children doing this activity on their own after several sessions.

This can be a very good way to work with two children who may have particular difficulty communicating with each other.

Decorating

Number of children: varies

Objectives:
1. Cooperative task completion
2. Improve communication skills
3. Body awareness
4. Self-esteem/affirmation
5. Foster altruistic behavior

Materials: Scarves, lengths of ribbon, fabric scraps, interesting clothes, etc.

Procedure: In our classroom, we keep a box of "stuff" in our closet. This box includes lengths of fabric, ribbon, yarn, glittery stuff, face paints, etc. Now and again, we adults have a day when we want to do something different for no particular reason. What we do then is decorate someone. (It's so hard to wait for Halloween!) Sometimes we choose a child who needs some special thing to happen to her that day. The different staff members all have their own favorite way of decorating. I, for example, like to use pipe cleaners and ponytail rubber bands to create hairdos that have tufts of hair standing up. Many of the children (boys sometimes more than girls) love to be decorated, but they rarely keep the decorations on for long. It is their choice as to how long or short a time they will remain decorated. I also try to give them choices while the process is going on, letting them direct me as to the final "look."

After this has been done by adults a few times, it can become a very productive group activity in which two or three children decorate someone. When using this as a group activity, you need to have a good adult-child ratio so that close supervision is possible. Encourage children to work together and to check frequently with the person they are decorating to ensure their continuing comfort and satisfaction.

Comments: An issue to stress is awareness of the other person's comfort. Children generally tend to be fairly tender with each other, but sometimes the excitement does carry them away. A good conclusion is to take pictures with a camera that provides instant pictures.

In order to avoid disappointment, try to allow enough time to get to everyone who wants a turn. This may run for several days.

Hot and Cold

Number of children: 5-15

Objectives:
1. Cooperative task completion
2. Improve communication skills
3. Analogy and consensus

Materials: None

Procedure: This game has probably been around as long as children have and can be a wonderful vehicle for bonding a group. It is essential that the adult monitor carefully and intervene so there is no failure. This involves abstract concepts and can be difficult for young children to grasp. You will need to do some preparatory work before doing the game with the group.

An object is selected that will be hidden. The adult should outline any areas that will be off-limits.

Explain that the object will be hidden and a player must seek it out. The job of the group is to guide the seeker by saying "hot" if he is getting near, and "cold" if he is moving away from the object. If there are two adults available, it may be a good idea to have one of the adults be the first seeker. The other adult can then guide the rest of the group in giving direction.

The seeker is sent out of the room while the object is hidden. You should attempt to get group agreement to choose the hiding place. Do not make it too difficult, as the attempt is not to frustrate the seeker, rather to work in unison with the person to help them find the object. When the object has been stashed, the seeker comes back into the room and begins the search.

The group verbally guides the seeker to the hiding place. Attempt to structure your time so that everyone who wishes can have a turn.

Group Splatter Paint

Number of children: 4-8

Objectives:
1. Cooperative task completion
2. Improve communication skills
3. Analogy/consensus

Materials: Newspapers, aprons or old shirts, runny paint in several colors (paint should be in containers that do not tip easily), paint brushes

Procedure: This activity needs to be done in an area that could stand a few splatters of paint. It is helpful to let parents know in advance that you will be doing this so they can make sure their children are dressed in old clothes.

Paint is applied to the paper by dipping the brush in paint, then whipping it about twelve inches above the paper. Explain to children that you are going to make a painting together in which all of you can take a part. I often spend some time looking at Jackson Pollock prints with them before we do this. Demonstrate the method, then ask children how they think they can avoid getting paint on each other. Discuss the necessity of being aware of the other children who are working with them.

Give each child one color of paint. You can have them move around the outside of the paper in order to get all colors in all areas.

You may choose to have the children trade colors with each other by negotiating.

Comments: An interesting if somewhat abstract idea to point out is that one color by itself creates a less interesting painting than the combination of colors formed by the contributions of different people.

This Ain't No Piano

Number of children: 5-12

Objectives:
1. Cooperative task completion
2. Body awareness

Materials: None

Procedure: Use a large space. Tell the children you want to build an instrument out of them. Ask one child to lie on the floor on her back. Ask her what her sound is. Explain that any sound she can make with her mouth is okay, but she needs to choose one that she can keep throughout the entire activity. Children catch on to this idea quickly, and you should be able to get quite a few interesting sounds.

Your objective is to add children until you have all of them placed. Children can be positioned lying next to each other or in a zig-zag shape with each child's head on the stomach of the previous one. As you add each child, have him demonstrate his sound.

When you have placed them all, tell them that you will now play the instrument. When you touch their foreheads they should make their sound as long as you are touching them. The adult should remain the conductor only for a short time and children should each have an opportunity to become the conductor.

Comments: For me, the optimum instrument is made with about five children. Often several will want to just watch until they see what you have done. Those children could then be included in a second instrument. Make sure each child who wishes has some chance to play the instrument. When this game is played repeatedly, children become very inventive with their sounds.

Going on a Trip

Number of children: 5-10

Objective: Affirmation. This activity is particularly well suited to allow children opportunities to scrutinize and talk about what they like about other children and to talk about their own needs and wants.

Materials: None

Procedure: This is a comfortable and quiet game. Ask the children to pretend that they are going on a trip. Tell them to close their eyes and imagine the trip. Then tell the following story or your own version of one like it. Try to be as honest about your own feelings as you can while doing this.

"We are going to go on a trip to a place far away from here, where it is warm and sunny, because I am tired of the rain. I am going to take all of you with me because you make me feel good and laugh and give good hugs. I am also going to take my mother with me because I get frightened when I am very far away from her for a long time. I am also going to take my daughter with us because I also like to have her with me a lot. I'm going to take my colored felt pens with me because I will want to draw pictures, and my camera because I will want to take photographs. I will also take my bathing suit because I will want to go swimming. We will go on a sailboat with a red sail and we will feel the wind in our hair and stay up late at night and watch the stars during our trip. Our trip will only take a week because we will have to come back so our friends and family don't miss us too much."

This story can continue on in a similar vein or be a very fantastic story about trips to the sun and the moon or anything else. The realness of the events in the story is not important, but the emotional honesty is.

When you have told your story, give the children turns to tell their story. You may have to help out by asking questions. Some sample questions are: Where would you like to go? How would you like to get there? What things would you like to take with you? Why do you want to take those things? Who would you like to take with you? Why?

This activity can be repeated many times—whenever you need a vacation!

This activity can also be used with only one child, providing an opportunity to get to know that child a little better and opening the door to discussions about some issues that may be troubling the child.

Mixed-up Puzzles

Number of children: 4-8

Objectives:
1. Cooperative task completion
2. Improve communication skills

Materials: Puzzles—the difficulty of the puzzle should be matched to the skill level of the individual child

Procedure: Have the children participating in the activity join you at a table. Round tables work well, as it makes it easy for all to reach the pieces they may need. Dump all the puzzle pieces out of the puzzles into one pile in the middle of the table. I had a regular routine worked out wherein I attempted to look like a two-year-old singing, "I love to make a mess . . ."

Give each child the frame of the puzzle you have selected for them. Deal the puzzle pieces out to the children in random order trying to make sure no child has more than a few of the pieces that belong to her puzzle.

Children must ask each other for a particular puzzle piece and should be encouraged to describe it in words rather than just pointing. You may need to help with this communication at times. The child who has the piece should give it to the person requesting it. Children quickly catch on to this and generally exhibit great delight in helping each other out.

Comments: This is an activity that children like to do more than once. We sometimes trade puzzles and do it again.

There is a tendency for the first one done to exclaim "I finished first. I win!" I simply respond by saying that it doesn't matter who finishes first, that what we are trying to do is to get all the puzzles back together.

Obstacle Course

Number of children: 6-16

Objectives:
1. Cooperative task completion
2. Improve communication skills
3. Body awareness

Materials: large space

Procedure: Have the children all stand or sit to one side while you explain what an obstacle course is. It may be helpful to have created one out of objects on some earlier occasion.

Explain that you will be making one but that you will be using people to create this one. You can demonstrate different ways that a person could be an obstacle. Have one child turn himself into an obstacle and explain to the next child that she will have to go under, over, around, or through that obstacle. The "obstacle" will tell her which way to go and must then assume a position which will make that possible. Some children will need assistance initially. The child who has gone through the first obstacle then becomes the second. Another child then goes through the two obstacles to become the third. Children may require help in spacing themselves so there is sufficient room to move without risking injury. When all the children have become obstacles, then the child who was the first goes through and to the side. Continue in this manner until the whole obstacle course is undone.

Comments: I like to have the "obstacle" asked about which way they would like people to go through—over, under, around, or through.

This activity is very popular and we often end up doing it several times in one activity period. A variation of this is to have pairs of children work together to create the obstacles.

Team Wrapping

Number of children: Depends on the number of adults available

Objectives:
1. Cooperative task completion
2. Improve communication
3. Preliminary activity

Materials: Item to be wrapped for each group, lightweight paper, ribbon, tape, scissors

Procedure: Work with children in teams of three or four. Give each team an item to be wrapped. I've always liked using stuffed animals.

Monitor each group to make sure that all members are involved in the activity and working cooperatively.

Comments: This activity should precede "Wrap a Friend."

A lightweight paper such as unprinted newsprint from roll ends works because it is easier for young children to manipulate than heavier papers.

Wrap a Friend

Number of children: Depends on the number of adults available

Objectives:
1. Cooperative task completion
2. Improve communication skills
3. Body awareness

Materials: Large sheets of newsprint from roll ends, masking tape

Procedure: Have children working in teams of four—three wrappers and one person to be wrapped. Good adult supervision is required. The object is for the team to wrap their person, paying close attention to the person's comfort at all times.

Each group gets a large space in which to work, several large sheets of paper, and masking tape. Remind them that they will need to communicate with the person they are wrapping to make sure that person is comfortable. *Have them leave the face free of wrapping.*

When the wrapping is all done and everyone has had a chance to admire it, the wrapped person gets to bust out (great fun)! All members of the group then help to clean up.

Comments: This game is a lot of fun, but it does have the potential for rowdiness, so there should be an adult for every two groups. The adult is there to tear off tape if the children need help, and to facilitate communication among the children in a group.

I strongly advise against the use of scissors in this activity.

Blanket Toss and Catch

Number of children: 6-10

Objectives:
1. Cooperative task completion
2. Improve communication skills
3. Analogy and consensus

Materials: Medium sized lightweight blanket or sheet, lightweight ball

Procedure: Spread the blanket out in a large space and have the children space themselves evenly around it. Have each child grasp the blanket firmly and toss the ball into the center. The object is to toss the ball into the air by lifting the blanket in unison.

Allow the children as much freedom as possible to figure out why it doesn't work quite right and help them to make adjustments either by shifting some of the children's positions or giving them a signal on which to toss.

Comments: This activity will probably provoke conflict when someone jerks the blanket too hard or too soon. You are there to help the children resolve the problem in a nonblaming and cooperative manner.

Clapping Names

Number of children: Any number

Objectives:
1. Improve communication skills
2. Self-esteem/affirmation

Materials: None

Procedure: The object is to clap one beat for each syllable in a child's name. Start with an explanation that different names have different numbers of syllables and you can clap to the syllables while chanting the name. I generally start with my own name and ask children if they would like their name done.

Clap once for each syllable while chanting the name. Generally, children will spontaneously join in with you. If not, encourage them to do so.

The activity can be varied by clapping loudly or softly.

Comments: This is a good activity for learning names in a new group or if there is a new child in the group. This can also be a good way to learn last names.

This works well as a warm-up for another group activity and is useful during transitions.

Because children feel strong ownership of their name and have a right to those feelings, it is very important to give them a choice about participating.

Musical Movement

Number of children: 10-18

Objectives:

1. Preliminary activity to "Musical Anythings"

Materials: Music, large space

Procedure: Explain to children that you will play some music, and while the music is playing, they may move. When the music stops, they must freeze and should not move again until the music starts again. Children who do not wish to participate should have a comfortable, safe place from which to observe.

When you are pretty sure the group has gotten the idea, you can complicate this game by having children do other things when the music stops. For example: sit down, lie down, kneel, stand on tiptoes, float slowly to the ground, etc. Allow children to make suggestions and remember that the sillier it is, the more fun it tends to be.

Comments: This activity works really well when there is one adult participating and one in charge of the music.

This activity, while valuable in its own right, is designed as a preliminary activity to "Musical Anythings" and with an older group, or one intimately schooled in the intricacies of "Musical Chairs," you may not need to spend much time with this particular game. As opposed to "Musical Chairs," in this game there are not any losers.

Musical Anythings

Number of children: 10-18

Objectives:
1. Cooperative task completion
2. Body awareness

Materials: Music, large space

Procedure: Do this activity in a large space with an area where nonparticipants can observe comfortably. Explain that just as before, when the music is on, they should move to the music. When it stops, they must find a partner, hold hands, and freeze. When this seems to be fairly well understood, give them alternative suggestions. Some examples: hold hands and sit down, give the other person a hug, rub noses with your partner, sit down so the bottoms of your feet are touching, touch elbows and freeze, touch tops of heads together, etc. Give children a chance to make suggestions as well. Talk about why a suggestion might not work if it seems too difficult, or if you do what the child has suggested and there has been a problem, talk about how you can change the suggestion to eliminate the problem.

Comments: This activity presents a certain degree of difficulty for young children, in that they must go from fairly fast and unconfined movement to one that involves the comfort of another person. Monitor carefully to avoid problems. You may also wish to suggest that children try to find a different partner each time if it seems that children are pairing off with the same person each time.

Drum and Sheet

Number of children: 10-18

Objective: Cooperative task completion

Materials: Large sheet, drum or other noisemaking instrument

Procedure: This activity needs to be done in a large space with relatively little intrusion of other noise.

Have the children all sit in a large circle, evenly spaced. One child goes to the middle of the circle and gets on hands and knees. Spread the sheet out over the child, with the child at the center. All other children must remain silent as the adult sneaks around and gives the drum to one child in the circle. That child beats the drum and the child under the sheet must crawl toward the drummer using the sound as a guide. This is actually easier than it sounds in spite of the giggles that result from the sight of the crawling sheet.

Comments: A light or white colored sheet works best as the child does not feel as confined as he would under a blanket or a sheet that lets in less light.

Rest assured that everyone will want a turn.

Filling up a Hug

Number of children: 10-20, depending on age

Objectives:
1. Involve children in a physical expression of affection
2. Demonstrate the rights of the individual to control what happens to his or her body
3. Help children become more aware of the subtle signals of comfort or discomfort in another person

Materials: None

Procedure: Use a space large enough for all children and the adult to sit in a circle. Before starting, explain to children that anyone may say whether they wish to be hugged or not. If a child passes, the hug is then given to the next child in the circle or back to the adult.

Say: "I have this little medium sized hug here and I would like to help it grow. I thought that if I passed the hug around this circle and each of you added some love to it, perhaps we can get it to be really big."

The adult then hugs the child next to her in the circle after checking to see if the child wishes to participate. Please note that this can be communicated verbally or not. Most children will, at this juncture, say yes. On receipt of the affirmative answer, the child then hugs the child next to them, and so on around the circle until the hug comes back to the adult. Often children will want to repeat this activity a number of times.

Sometimes this activity is a good quick one to do before doing other group work, as it creates cohesiveness in the group. It also allows children who are uncomfortable initiating physical demonstrations of affection the opportunity to partake in some hugging and touching.

IV
Appendix

Bibliography

This is by no means a complete list of all the resources available. It should, however, provide enough listings to enable you to get further information in your area of interest.

Parenting or teaching for peace and justice

Alternative Celebrations Catalogue. Alternatives, PO Box 1707, Forest Park, GA: Pilgrim Press, 1982.

Ronald C. Arnett. *Dwell in Peace: Applying Nonviolence to Everyday Relationships*. Elgin, IL: Brethren Press, 1980.

Nancy Carlsson-Page and Diane Levin. *Helping Young Children Understand Peace, War and the Nuclear Threat*. Washington, DC: National Association for the Education of Young Children, 1985.

Kate Cloud, et al. *Watermelons not War! A Support Book for Parenting in the Nuclear Age*. Philadelphia: New Society Publishers, 1984.

Virginia Coover, Ellen Deacon, Charles Esser, and Christopher Moore. *Resource Manual for a Living Revolution*. Philadelphia: New Society Publishers, 1985.

Lois Dorn. *Peace in the Family, a Workbook of Ideas and Actions*. New York: Pantheon Books, 1983.

Rudolf Dreikurs. *Family Council: The Dreikurs Technique for Putting an End to War Between Parents and Children (and Between Children and Children)*. Chicago: Henry Regnery, 1974.

Adele Farber and Elaine Mazlich. *Liberated Parents/Liberated Children*. New York: Grosset and Dunlap, 1974.

Jacqueline Haessly. *Peacemaking: Family Activities for Justice and Peace*. New York: Paulist Press, 1980.

Stephanie Judson, ed. *A Manual on Nonviolence and Children*. Philadelphia: New Society Publishers, 1984.

Barbara Kuczen. *Childhood Stress*. New York: Delacorte Press, 1982.

James and Kathleen McGinnis. *Parenting for Peace and Justice*. Maryknoll, NY: Orbis Books, 1981.

Kathleen McGinnis and Barbara Oehlberg. *Starting Out Right: Nurturing Young Children as Peacemakers*. Yorktown Heights, NY: Meyer Stone Books, 1988.

M. Montessori. *Education and Peace*. Chicago: Henry Regnery Press, 1972.

J. Lorne Peachey. *How to Teach Peace to Children*. Scottdale, PA: Herald Press, 1981.

Priscilla Prutzman, et.al., The Children's Creative Response to Conflict Program. *The Friendly Classroom for a Small Planet: A Handbook on Creative Approaches to Living and Problem Solving for Children*. Philadelphia: New Society Publishers, 1988.

Sue Spayth Riley. *How to Generate Values in Young Children*. Washington, DC: National Association for the Education of Young Children, 1984.

Virginia Satir. *Peoplemaking*. Palo Alto, CA: Science and Behavior Books, 1972.

Michael Shulman and Eva Mekler. *Bringing Up a Moral Child: A New Approach for Teaching Your Child to be Kind, Just and Responsible*. Reading, MA: Addison Wesley, 1985.

Sidney B. Simon and Sally Wendkos Olds. *Helping Your Child Learn Right from Wrong: A Guide to Values Clarification*. New York: Simon & Schuster, 1976.

Howard Tolley, Jr. *Children and War: Political Socialization to International Conflict*. New York: Teachers College Press, 1973.

Try This: Family Adventures Toward Shalom. Nashville, TN: Discipleship Resources, 1979.

William and Mary Van Ornum. *Talking to Children About Nuclear War*. New York: Scribner, 1984.

Miscellaneous teaching resources

Jim Blake and Barbara Ernst. *The Great Perpetual Learning Machine*. Boston and Toronto: Little, Brown and Co., 1976.

Sue Bredekamp, ed. *Developmentally Appropriate Practice*. Washington, DC: National Association for the Education of Young Children, 1987.

Rachel Carr. *Be a Frog, a Bird or a Tree: Creative Yoga Exercises for Children*. New York: Colophon Books, 1973.

Lynn Ocone. *The Youth Gardening Book*. Burlington, VT: Gardens for All, 1983.

Letty Cottin Pogrebin, ed. *Stories for Free Children*. New York: McGraw Hill, 1982.

Eliminating gender bias

Carrie Carmichael. *Non-sexist Childraising*. Boston: Beacon Press, 1977.

Monroe D. Cohen, ed. *Growing Free: Ways to Help Children Overcome Sex-role Stereotypes*. Washington, DC: Association for Childhood Education International, 1976.

Selma Greenberg. *Right from the Start: A Guide to Nonsexist Childrearing*. Boston: Houghton Mifflin, 1978.

Letty Cottin Pogrebin. *Growing Up Free: Raising Your Child in the Eighties*. New York: McGraw Hill, 1980.

Multicultural approaches

American Friends Service Committee and International Recreation Association. *Games Enjoyed by Children Around the World*. Washington, DC: Association for Childood Education International, 1970.

Frances E. Kendall. *Diversity in the Classroom*. New York: Teachers College Press, 1983.

C. K. Rekdal and B. S. L. Kan. *Jing Ho Hauk Ho: Chinese Activity Book*. Seattle, WA: Fortune Cookie Press, 1976.

Olivia N. Saracho and Bernard Spodek, eds. *Understanding the Multicultural Experience in Early Childhood Education*. Washington, DC: National Association for the Education of Young Children, 1983.

Noncompetitive approaches

Andrew Fluegelman. *The New Games Book*. New York: Dolphin Books, 1976.

Alfie Kohn. *No Contest: The Case Against Competition*. Boston: Houghton Mifflin, 1986.

Terry Orlick. *Every Kid Can Win*. Chicago: Nelson-Hall, 1977.

Terry Orlick. *The Cooperative Sports and Games Book: Challenge Without Competition*. New York: Pantheon Books, 1978.

Articles and booklets

Margie Carter and Noel Menadier. "The Caregiver as Citizen of the World." *Beginnings*, Spring 1986.

Norma R. Law. "Children and War." A position paper for the Association for Childhood Education International, 1973.

"What Shall We Tell the Children?" Booklet for Parents. Parenting in a Nuclear Age, c/o Bananas, 6501 Telegraph Avenue, Oakland, CA 94609.

Some Children's Books

While far from all-inclusive, the following list was generated in one year of teaching. I encourage you to make such a list for yourself so you can remember books you like.

Max Bollinger. *The Lonely Prince*. New York: Methuen Children's Books, 1981.
This is a positive story with great illustrations about a young prince who has everything but a friend. Its main message is about caring. We deleted one page that mentions toy soldiers—but we're fanatics!

Tomie De Paola. *The Legend of the Bluebonnet: An Old Tale of Texas*. New York: Putnam Publishing Group, 1983.
This is a Commanche/Texan folktale about a young girl who sacrifices her most prized possession for the good of her people. There are elements of this story that generated lengthy discussion among staff.

Barbara Douglass. *The Great Town and Country Bicycle Balloon Chase*. New York: Lothrop, 1984.
A wonderful and realistic adventure story about a girl and her grandfather. The drawings are beautiful and it is a good alternative to violent adventure stories.

Joan Drescher. *Your Family, My Family*. New York: Walker, 1980.
Great book. Deals with all kinds of families, multicultural, and no stereotypes.

Marie Hall Ets. *Elephant in a Well*. New York: Viking, 1972.
A young elephant falls into a well, and a cooperative effort is required to get her out. This has the same message as the *Enormous Turnip* story, but is illustrated with woodcuts.

Marie Hall Ets. *Gilberto and the Wind*. New York: Viking, 1963.
A young Chicano boy plays with the wind. This is a gentle story.

Jean Craighead George. *All Upon a Stone*. New York: Crowell, 1971.
Realistic portrayal of the life around a rock. The pictures are lovely and the book conveys a strong sense of respect for living things.

Laura Greene. *Help: Getting to Know About Needing and Giving*. New York: Human Sciences Press, 1981.
This is a superlative book about getting help from tools and people, and about the giving of help.

Barbara S. Hazen. *Even If I Did Something Awful?* New York: Macmillan, 1981.
A young girl's mother assures her she will love her no matter what. This book shows the feelings of the adult with great sensitivity.

Ole Hertz. *Tobias Has a Birthday*. Minneapolis, MN: Carolrhoda Books, 1984.
Story of a boy who lives in Greenland. A very good portrayal of life in another culture that children can relate to.

Amy Hest. *The Crack of Dawn Walkers*. New York: Macmillan, 1984.
A girl and her grandfather go for an early morning walk. Deals with the issue of having to share someone you love, and portrays the grandfather honestly.

Lyn Littlefield Hoopes. *When I Was Little*. New York: E. P. Dutton, 1983.
Wonderful, loving conversation between a child and her mother who has a younger child.

Mildred Kantrowitz. *Maxie*. New York: Macmillan, 1980.
An old woman who lives alone doesn't think anyone needs her. Her neighbors show her that she is wrong.

Joan Lesikin. *Down the Road*. Englewood Cliffs, NJ: Prentice-Hall, 1978.
A turtle and a snake look for a home together. This story is about sharing.

Ada B. Litchfield. *A Button in Her Ear*. Niles, IL: Albert Whitman Concept Books, 1976.
A girl must get a hearing aid. Depicts the misunderstanding that can arise from hearing loss. Very positive and depicts women and minorities well.

Miyoko Matsutani, trans. by Alvin Tresselt. *The Witch's Magic Cloth*. New York: Parents Magazine Press, 1969.
This is a Japanese folktale in which a witch, feared to be wicked, turns out to be quite friendly and generous. The heroine in this story is an elderly woman.

Ann McGovern. *Little Wolf*. New York: Scholastic, 1970.
A Native American boy who doesn't wish to learn to hunt becomes a healer instead.

Betty Miles. *Around and Around—Love*. New York: Random House, 1975.
Simple text about love and feelings with evocative photographs of people.

Helen Oxenbury. *The Great Big Enormous Turnip*. New York: Franklin Watts, 1968.
A traditional European folktale in which the message is obvious—teamwork works, and even the smallest has something to contribute.

Maxine B. Rosenberg. *Being Adopted*. New York: Lothrop, 1984.
Deals with several adoptive children from another culture, across race lines. Deals honestly with feelings children may have.

Maxine B. Rosenberg. *My Friend Leslie: The Story of a Handicapped Child*. New York: Lothrop, 1983.
Very wonderful book about a handicapped girl and her kindergarten friend. Good black and white photographs. Honest and positive.

Amy Schwartz. *Begin at the Beginning*. New York: Trophy Picture Books, 1984.
A girl tries to paint a wonderful picture of the universe and learns that it is made of small daily things.

Ann H. Scott. *On Mother's Lap*. New York: McGraw Hill, 1972.
This is a story about a young boy whose mother has an infant child. This is a simple, quiet story about feelings, with a very matter-of-fact approach to the Eskimo culture.

Norma Simon. *Nobody's Perfect, Not Even My Mother*. Niles, IL: Albert Whitman Concept Books, 1981.
The message of this book is that every one is good at something. It presents nontraditional male and female roles.

Harris A. Stone. *The Last Free Bird*. Englewood Cliffs, NJ: Prentice-Hall, 1967.
An interesting and alarming book about human exploitation of the environment.

Barbara Williams. *Kevin's Grandma*. New York: E. P. Dutton, 1978.
Two grandmothers are presented in this book, a very traditional one, and another that leads an unusual life. The message clearly presented is acceptance of different lifestyles.

Vera B. Williams. *Three Days on a River in a Red Canoe*. New York: Greenwillow Books, 1984.
A child, cousin, mother, and aunt go on a canoe trip. This is an enjoyable and realistic story.

Diane Wolkstein. *The Banza*. New York: Macmillan, 1987.
This is a Haitian folktale about a goat and a tiger who befriend each other, and who, even though they are kept apart by their differences, retain some benefits of their friendship.

Other Resources and Groups

Arts Resources for Cooperation
Sarah Pirtle
54 Thayer Road
Greenfield, MA 01301

Association for Childhood Education International
3615 Wisconsin Avenue NW
Washington, DC 20016

Center on War and the Child
PO Box 487
Eureka Springs, AR 72632
This group has a newsletter as well as other materials available.

Children's Defense Fund
122 C Street NW
Washington, DC 20001

Concerned Educators Allied for a Safe Environment
17 Gerry Street
Cambridge, MA 02138

Educators for Social Responsibility
639 Massachusetts Avenue
Cambridge, MA 02139

Family Pastimes
R.R. 4
Perth, Ontario
Canada K7H 3C6
Source for cooperative games.

Information Center on Children's Cultures
UNICEF
331 East 38th Street
New York, NY 10016
A wealth of materials available for use in multicultural teaching.

Lollipop Power
PO Box 1171
Chapel HIll, NC 27514
Publishes alternative children's books including books about gay and lesbian families.

National Association for the Education of Young Children
1834 Connecticut Avenue NW
Washington, DC 20009
Many publications available.

National Coalition on Television Violence
PO Box 2157
Champaign, IL 61820

National Parenting for Peace and Justice Network
Institute for Peace and Justice
4144 Lindell Boulevard, No. 400
St. Louis, MO 63108

New Seed Press
PO Box 3016
Stanford, CA 94305
Publishes children's books free from racial, class, or sex role stereotyping.

Parenting Press
7750 31st Avenue NE, Suite 200
Seattle, Washington 98115
Publishes books for parents that deal with positive discipline and problem-solving.

Parents and Teachers for Social Responsibility
64 Main Street
Montpelier, VT 05602

Peace Project/Camp Fire Inc.
4601 Madison Avenue
Kansas City, MO 64112

World Council for Curriculum and Instruction
Maxine Dunfee, Secretariat
School of Education
Indiana University
Bloomington, IN 47405

Notes

More Resources from New Society Publishers

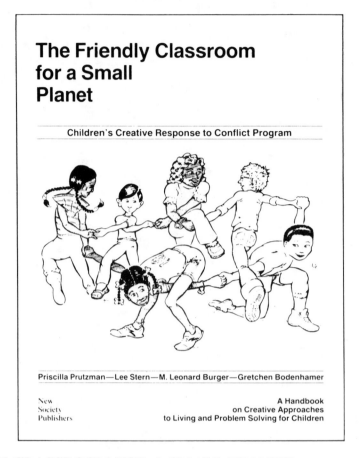

THE FRIENDLY CLASSROOM FOR A SMALL PLANET

by Priscilla Prutzman, Lee Stern, M. Leonard Burger, & Gretchen Bodenhamer
Children's Creative Response to Conflict Program

The possibility of peace begins close at hand. To provide some measure of hope and security for our children, we must work with them to build peace and harmony *where they are:* at home, in school, with their friends.

    Believing that creative response to conflict requires more than conflict resolution skills, the Children's Creative Response to Conflict program addresses the roots of conflict and violence, offering teachers, group leaders, and parents perspectives, techniques, and tools developed and refined in a wide variety of settings—from inner-city to small-town schools, with children's and leaders' groups—over a period of fifteen years. *The Friendly Classroom for a Small Planet* includes hundreds of exercises, activities, methods, and tips designed to nurture self-esteem, build cooperation and community, develop effective communication (including listening, observing, and speaking skills), promote both self-awareness and empathy, and train effective conflict resolution skills (like negotiation and roleplaying).

    The Friendly Classroom for a Small Planet is an essential sourcebook for any teacher, parent, or adult leader trying to create a cooperative and supportive learning environment for children.

144 pages. Illustrations. Charts. Index.

For current prices, to order, or to receive New Society Publisher's complete catalogue, call or write:

In the United States:	*In Canada:*
New Society Publishers	New Society Publishers
4527 Springfield Ave.	P.O Box 189
Philadelphia, PA 19143	Gabriola Island, BC V0R 1X0
(800) 333-9093	(800) 567-6772